The Politics
of Debt

Essays and Interviews

The Politics of Debt

Essays and Interviews

Sjoerd van Tuinen
and Arjen Kleinherenbrink

Winchester, UK
Washington, USA

JOHN HUNT PUBLISHING

First published by Zero Books, 2020
Zero Books is an imprint of John Hunt Publishing Ltd., No. 3 East St., Alresford,
Hampshire SO24 9EE, UK
office@jhpbooks.com
www.johnhuntpublishing.com
www.zero-books.net

For distributor details and how to order please visit the 'Ordering' section on our website.

Text copyright: Sjoerd van Tuinen & Arjen Kleinherenbrink 2018

ISBN: 978 1 78904 228 3
978 1 78904 229 0 (ebook)
Library of Congress Control Number: 2018961986

A CIP catalogue record for this book is available from the British Library.

Design: Stuart Davies

UK: Printed and bound by CPI Group (UK) Ltd, Croydon, CR0 4YY
US: Printed and bound by Thomson-Shore, 7300 West Joy Road, Dexter, MI 48130

We operate a distinctive and ethical publishing philosophy in
all areas of our business, from our global network of authors to
production and worldwide distribution.

Contents

The "Financial" Crisis: Ten Years Later

Arjen Kleinherenbrink and Sjoerd van Tuinen

The crisis and its roots

Capitalism has always had its crises. This time, the crisis began in the United States. Mesmerized by a booming housing market and high demand for mortgage-backed securities in financial markets, lenders had started issuing vast numbers of mortgages to borrowers with bad credit scores and low incomes. These subprime loans soon became the main ingredient of mortgage bundles that were traded on the open market. Such "collateralized debt obligations" (CDOs) would normally consist of diversified debt, so that defaults on high risk loans would be compensated by continued payments on reliable loans. By 2006, however, these packages were dominated by high risk subprime mortgage debt. Credit-rating agencies nonetheless kept awarding CDOs the coveted triple A status, which reinforced the belief that subprime mortgages were safe and sound investments.

We all know what happened next. The housing market peaked, house prices started to drop, and borrowers started to default. In 2007 and 2008, the ensuing subprime crisis dragged the United States and many other countries into the Great Recession, the worst financial catastrophe since the 1930s. In the wake of this, a European debt crisis erupted in 2009. Several EU countries found themselves unable to repay their government debt and were forced to bail out their banks with taxpayer money and credit from the infamous "Troika" – the European Commission, the European Central Bank and the International Monetary Fund. It was then decided that austerity politics would offer the fastest road to recovery, a decision that many of those responsible now openly regret. At the time, however, EU member states either volunteered or were coerced to drastically reduce government spending. Public services, social safety nets and education as well as healthcare systems took the brunt of the impact in the form of massive budget cuts, privatization and defunding.

These crises were not isolated incidents. Their size and impact notwithstanding, they are but symptoms of deeper, structural problems inherent to the neoliberal politics and economics that have been in the ascendant since the Reagan and Thatcher years. As scholars such as David Harvey and Wolfgang Streeck remind us, our current political and economic situation must be interpreted in light of a "class compromise" that ended in the 1970s.[1] After the Second World War, the Western world agreed to make capitalism operate in conjunction with social democracy. There would be free markets for the pursuit of profit and accumulation of wealth, but states would intervene in those markets in the interest of keeping the social peace. Hence the emergence of the welfare state: a balancing mechanism to compensate the indifference of markets with a measure of social justice and wealth redistribution. This seemed to work for several decades, until economic growth collapsed in the 1970s.

For Harvey, what followed was a power grab, as economic elites and ruling classes got nervous and moved to protect their own interests, thereby ushering in a renewed phase of class struggle. According to Streeck, a "golden age" of capitalism, with indefinitely increasing wealth for owners and workers alike, ended in the 1970s. The new reality was characterized by the mutually reinforcing tendencies of declining growth, mounting debt and increasing inequality. Neoliberalism emerged as a series of attempts (including experiments with inflation, public and government debts, and new financial products) to overcome these problems. Free markets were allowed to colonize and commodify increasingly large parts of our private lives, public institutions, planetary resources and of course money and credit themselves (the so-called "financialization" – or liquefaction/liquidation – of debts), based on the belief that capitalism

2

would start delivering on its promises if only it were allowed to expand everywhere. Unsurprisingly, the result was more declining growth (save for the happy few), increasing inequality and growing debt, which turned out to be *structural* and not *incidental* features of our socio-economical arrangements.[2] The recent crises, then, result in part from the continued application of a solution that in fact only exacerbates the problem.

Yet neoliberalism is more than renewed struggle in a globalized and financialized world – the prefix *neo* is wholly deserved. Philip Mirowski, for example, has asked how it is possible that the very elites and institutions that caused a global financial catastrophe are not just still in power, but have even managed to consolidate their positions.[3] Mirowski's hypothesis is that many of us – particularly economists – now suffer from anxiety-inducing cognitive dissonance, which we remedy by reinterpreting the failures of capitalist doctrine as if they were confirmations of its truth. Mirowski further identifies a "neoliberal thought collective," centered around the infamous Mont Pèlerin Society, which actively feeds the world such reinterpretations.

A distinct feature of neoliberalism is its reengineering of the state into an instrument to actively shape citizens into individualistic entrepreneurs of the self, contra more classical approaches according to which people would "naturally" behave as self-interested utility maximizers, so that the state merely had to step back in order for free markets to flourish.[4] If financial elites have learned anything, it is that states are incredibly useful tools to help their interests survive a crisis while ordinary citizens suffer. Although generally kept at bay by the powerful, states have suddenly become necessary to reestablish order and save the banks. This illustrates how under neoliberalism, crisis itself is actively wielded as a tool by corporate and financial elites.[5]

What we are dealing with are therefore not just financial

3

crises, but structural effects that concern the political systems and social fabric of entire countries. There is a bitter irony in using the term "financial crisis" in relation to 2007 and 2008, as it is precisely finance that has emerged largely unscathed and – as we will see – continues to operate as it has for decades, while the repercussions for societies and states have been enormous and irreversible. This raises a first type of question: What are the proper points of application to improve the current economic and political order? If the crisis is rooted in deep structural features of our social system, then the implementation of slightly stricter regulation here and some ethical codes of conduct there is laughable – even though this is, by and large, what the response to the Great Recession and Eurozone crisis has come down to. The problem is that there is no real alternative on the table: there is no New Deal or Keynesian strategy with sufficient political and popular support, and no actor powerful enough for its large-scale implementation.

Populism and politics

When the Eurozone crisis began, people were encouraged not to overthink things. The crisis was portrayed as an accident (albeit a sizable one), as something that definitely did not express systematic problems. The "lazy Greeks" simply had not paid their bills, or such was the narrative frame that conceived of national economies as isomorphic to household finances. Officials like Jeroen Dijsselbloem donned the mantle of stern bookkeepers that would swoop in to save the EU from the Greeks and the Greeks from themselves. When it turned out that Italy, Spain, Portugal and Ireland were also full of lazy Greeks, the EU started to save them as well.

Trying to pass the crisis off as a merely arithmetical affair of collecting some overdue payments did not succeed. Instead, the crisis painfully ruptured a political and economic fault line that runs roughly between the northern and southern members of the

Eurozone. Briefly put, economic growth in southern countries is mainly driven by domestic demand, whereas northern countries mainly realize growth via exports. Because of this difference, any economic measure (for example, fixing exchange rates or devaluing currency) can potentially be beneficial to the North while spelling disaster for the South, and vice versa.[6] The German-led North has the upper hand in the resulting power dynamic. When the crisis hit, devaluation of the euro would likely have allowed the South to restore competitiveness, but this was not an attractive option for the North. The South was forced to implement disastrous austerity measures instead. For countries like Greece, the economic future now looks bleak because of this. Hollowed out by austerity politics and even more dependent on the EU's "good graces," each new crisis will see such countries rely on further credit and bailouts from the North, a situation that is ultimately highly undesirable for both regions. Unsurprisingly, scholars and politicians from across the political spectrum have started to argue that these countries might be better off without the euro, in order to escape what is essentially debt bondage on a geopolitical level.

A second rupture that emerged with the crisis lies not between countries, but between elites and "ordinary citizens." The raucous reawakening of populism is easily the most politically significant result of the crisis. The election of Donald Trump, Brexit and the rise of populist parties in Europe and elsewhere all signal the bankruptcy of the belief that free markets and globalization will be beneficial to all. As this illusion was shattered, center-Left parties were dealt a tremendous electoral blow. In previous decades, they had made themselves the figureheads of the idea that even ordinary workers would benefit from economic globalization, and of the notion that free-market thinking was "pragmatic" or "realistic" as opposed to "outdated" leftist ideals. After the crisis, they had to pay the price for "shaking off [their] ideological feathers," which the

Dutch Labor prime minister Wim Kok could still proudly call a "liberating experience" back in 1995.

The new populism is partially directed against "the system." It rails against the power and indifference of banks, multinationals, EU technocrats and corporate lobbies. It calls for an end to the ceaseless depoliticization of the public interest into the schemes of international finance. It demands a restoration of the sovereignty of nations and the dignity of citizens that has been undone or rendered impotent by distant transnational governments and the cold logic of the market. Yet the new populism does not just concern itself with bureaucratic and economic affronts. Were this the case, then it might have died down once economies started to recover. Instead, the new populism lashes out against anything associated with the intrusion of the wider world into local communities, against anything that denies people stability and sovereignty in social, economic, political and religious affairs. The new populism therefore also has it out for immigrants, feminists, Muslims and for a host of progressive ideas that it claims have facilitated economic and cultural displacement ever since the 1960s. Again, there is a bitter irony to this focus on identity and ideology instead of material causes. While it serves populism's dire need for intellectual cachet, it does not take a genius to see that, for example, the loss of industrial jobs in Western nations and economic migration to those same countries can be traced back to the same root causes, all pertaining to globalized capitalism. Yet instead of solidarity, the prevailing response is hostility toward the "Other" who threatens what little one has left after decades of globalization.

A recurring strand of thought in this new populism is the idea that once all sorts of "cultural problems" are fixed, economic prosperity will automatically return. In many countries, populism therefore leans toward the (identitarian) right side of the political spectrum, and it is indeed the political Right that seems to profit most from the reestablishment of mass popular outrage as a political force. Nevertheless, scholars like Ernesto Laclau and Chantal Mouffe have argued that now is also the time for a left-wing populism that incorporates various struggles against economic oppression and cultural discrimination.[7] Such a populism might have a real chance in Latin America and Southern Europe, but in countries such as the UK and the US, the Left currently still seems to be too internally divided for this to occur.

These two ruptures, one between North and South and the other between the 1 percent and the "ordinary people," are the fault lines of a global political struggle concerning debt, dependence, identity and sovereignty. This continuing struggle cannot be neatly divided into separate economic, political and social components. This raises a second type of question. How can we once again start thinking and acting as *political* economists, rather than just as economists who pretend that the world is a ledger? How to restore financial security, cultural stability and political sovereignty to ordinary citizens? Is there an alternative to the Scylla of continued globalization and the Charybdis of reactionary nationalism? What of the role of states, transnational governments and the many experiments with direct democracy in all this?

The inertia of finance

Roughly a decade after the crisis, we see that the financial world is even stronger than before. As an article in *The Economist* puts it: "Anyone who fell asleep in 2006 and woke up to look at the financial markets today would have no idea there had ever been a crisis."[8] In many places, share prices are soaring, interests are low, unemployment is low and investor confidence is high. As long as one selectively ignores the regions struck hardest by the crisis and the ensuing austerity politics, everyone seems to be doing well. Except, of course, for the increasing precarization of labor, the hollowing out of pensions, and a few other things that only a spoilsport would bring up in joyous times of economic recovery.

The financial world has regained its self-confidence and, as such, has returned to its pre-crisis modus operandi. The world is once again operating at record levels of corporate, household, government and investor debt. Subprime mortgages are still hot commodities, the only difference being that they have been rebranded "nonprime" or "complex prime" loans for borrowers with "less-than-perfect" credit. The derivatives market is also doing well, amounting to 700 trillion dollars in 2013 (which is several times the size of the world economy). Yet it is hardly any more transparent than it was before the crisis, and this, too, is highly problematic. We should recall that one of the main reasons that trading and lending froze after the fall of Lehman Brothers in 2008 was that the derivatives market was so opaque that nobody could tell which other parties were also teetering on the edge. The Trump administration, however, has chosen to partially repeal the 2010 Dodd-Frank Wall Street Reform and Consumer Protection Act, which was designed to improve the US financial regulatory environment and shore up consumer protection. Dozens of US banks are now exempt from Dodd-Frank Act regulations.

In Europe, banks are lending around 90 percent of their equity – less than the 95-98 percent of equity sometimes lent before the crisis, but nowhere near a more sensible scenario in which banks would hold at least 20 percent of their assets. The larger banks can still operate on the premise that once things go south, they will be bailed out because they are "too big to fail." It seems to be a fact of modern life that the traditional association of debt with morality (as expressed by the German word *Schuld*) may be valid for individuals or states, but is simply nonexistent for these large institutions. Their every act must be forgiven, because they are considered vital components of our economic infrastructures. This was proven once again in 2017, when the European Central Bank and the Italian state bailed out the Banca Monte dei Paschi di Siena, the oldest bank in the world. The same infernal dilemma thus still haunts regulators: either use public funds to rescue a malperforming institution, or risk a bank run with catastrophic consequences.

Meanwhile, financial elites have learned that global crisis, political turmoil and popular outrage barely cause them any harm. The Global Recession and Eurozone crisis have had few legal consequences for those operating at the pinnacle of financial power. Some of them may have broken a sweat during the LuxLeaks, SwissLeaks, Panama Papers and Paradise Papers publications, but by now they must have realized that shady offshore accounts and tax evasion, too, are simply accepted as yet another depressing fact of life by the general public.

All this testifies to an incredible degree of resilience and inertia in individual financial institutions as well as the financial system as a whole (not to mention regulatory agencies and political bodies). The aftermath of the crisis proves beyond doubt that they are what philosophers used to call "practico-inert beings" and nowadays refer to as "hyperobjects": abstract entities that loom large over everyday life, that often barely change even while their environment is in great turmoil, and that overtly and covertly make vast amounts of people maintain and even strengthen them – even if "feeding the beast" is against their own interests. All of us participate in this system, whether it be through our mortgages, savings accounts, pension funds, medical insurance or even school tuition (even "public" universities are now often eager to engage in financial speculation[9]). This raises a third and final type of question. If even the worst economic crisis that the world has seen in 80 years brings about no change to our economic system, and if almost everyone is actively participating in and dependent on this system, then what, exactly, are our options for the future?

This volume

The main theme, the raison d'être, of this book is the observation, shared by many, that in the wake of the large-scale processes of depoliticization – financialization, juridification, bureaucratization and moralization – it is increasingly unclear what the democratic potency of the oft-called "public sphere" might be. How can public interest be represented and articulated in the face of technocratic governance, populist politics or corporate power protected by supranational regulation?

The financialization of the global economy since the 1970s divides collective debt into increasingly asymmetrical relations between individuals, states and financial bureaucracies, leading to ever-narrower margins in which political decisions are made. We are witnessing an infinite piling of financial debts whose servicing requires ever more money, more loans, more speculation, more growth and more risk. Both at the level of the state and at the level of private households, this has led to a rapid loss of sovereignty, as well as the destruction of finite hard assets and real productivity. States become more and more dependent on market finance and securitized credit, such that the distinction between public and private debt and the relation between indebtedness and the common good tend to disappear. Socio-economic life is increasingly subject to debt bondage, as we are becoming self-entrepreneurs with study debts, mortgage debts, consumer debts and credit-ratings that compel us to keep digging and filling the debt hole ever faster. All these processes of de-democratization are themselves deeply political. How, then, can the issue of debt be reclaimed by all its stakeholders?

Instead of a financial crisis, what seems to be at stake is a crisis of sovereignty and of what we consider to be an emancipated citizen – in other words, a social and political crisis. But even if debt is at the heart of this crisis, being both its cause and sometimes its cure, it hardly ever appears as a political issue. And even when it does, questions of political economy are quickly covered and subdued under an intricate blend of financial-economic "laws" and archaic moralizations (e.g. about Greece as the "villain" and the European Union as the "savior"). For example, where philosophers and anthropologists have long insisted on the inseparability of the financial and moral aspects of debt, contemporary public discourse does exactly the reverse. It obfuscates questions such as who controls institutions and structures and who has the power to create them or reshape them to their own ends. Instead it pairs an objective rationality (debt as fact of nature) with a subjective sentimentality (debt as guilt), redefining social reality and citizenship in terms of precarity, private property, market, and the spectacle of inequality.

In the essays and interviews in this volume, economists and philosophers try to increase our understanding of the various questions raised here. This is especially important given that, more than a decade after the crisis, scholars, journalists and politicians alike agree that it is not a matter of *if*, but *when* the next crisis will hit. Everybody agrees that with the last crisis, we missed a "real opportunity" for systemic change. As we approach the inevitable next crisis, we have two options. The first is cynicism: to know that everybody knows that something must change, but to also know that nobody will act on that knowledge. The second involves action, and action requires that we keep increasing our understanding of the real structure of our political and economic order, that we identify the intimate relations between economic, political and social concerns, and that we explore possible alternatives to what is currently our economic future – which looks bleak except for those who are already rich.

1. Debts and Interests from the Perspective of the General Economy

Émilie Bernier
University of Ottawa

Among the many criticisms that have been raised about the consequences of indebtedness, some have pointed out that a myriad of possible patterns for creditor-debtor relationships existed long before our forms of economic obligations were developed. Indeed, while indebtedness, both private and public or sovereign, has undeniably become one of the most pressing of contemporary problems around the world, one must recognize that the social prevalence of debt is not for that matter an exclusive feature of these neoliberal times. It can be tempting, consequently, to nourish the critical imagination with examples drawn from anthropological literature about gift economies and other such systems of symbolic and ritual exchange. In what follows, I assess the value of such political imaginations that claim some alternative notion of interest might be used to bolster resistance to the injustice concealed in current legal debt contracts. Analyzing previous arrangements of payback obligations, one realizes that they responded to incentives that are not unlike those animating contemporary structures of indebtedness, namely a social demand for tempering and controlling individual desires, lives and powers. I would argue, in fact, that there exists no notion of interest, utility or value that is not subject to the costs and consequences of such a fundamental economy of power. Hopefully, this will provide us with a better perspective from which to explore aspects of our own historical formation, and to understand the true challenge of contemporary regimes of indebtedness.

The current credit system, indeed, is not intended to

facilitate the allotment of productive investments, as we might legitimately expect. Financial companies seem much less interested in throwing *funds* into circulation and allowing those funds to increase the value of available goods. Rather, they appear motivated mainly by the maximizing of profits through their granting of a maximum number of loans. Such a credit frenzy might have represented nothing more than a fancy twist on modern-day profit-making had it not been so blatantly shown, in 2008, to depend on the suffering of the most vulnerable populations.

To add insult to injury, public money was then used to bail out the banking system that had profited from such machinations. Public budgets have been starkly impacted by such rescue operations, and the consequential re-allotment of fiscal revenues made a wide range of acquired social rights all the more precarious. Thus, where neoliberal budgetary policies have been implemented, it is increasingly the burden of every member of the public to provide for his or her own education, health care and housing. Formerly *"droits-créances,"* as they were called in French – literally "right-debts," or "entitlements" allowing the citizens of a state to experience the freedoms granted to them by their constitutions – these public debts have tended to become mere *créances*, that is to say, personal debts.

These facts altogether justify the feeling that the current level of indebtedness is, in many ways, detrimental to social well-being. In the Eurozone and in Great Britain, austerity politics have been widely criticized, and many have pointed to the resulting mental health issues and, in some cases, even suicide.[1] Since 2012, the Italian *Vedove Bianche* – literally, the "White Widows" – have been protesting against the fiscal obligations that, allegedly, led their husbands to take their own lives.[2] Debt, in such cases, represents "a social levy whose price is life itself."[3]

Debts are a part of the neoliberal social machinery that can quite rightly be regarded as a means of incapacitation and exclusion. One might think that debts are an incidental feature of modern societies. However, there is an abundant body of literature arguing that the prevalence and importance of debts, far from merely indicating an historical anomaly and a cause of social disintegration, have always and everywhere defined the basic condition of all societies.[4] Influenced by Marcel Mauss' *The Gift*[5] – itself an essay on the obligation to *return* as much as on an alleged propensity to *give* – French sociology has been nourished by an important discussion on non-utilitarian forms of reciprocity.[6] Moreover, recent contributions to economic anthropology have argued that in the most ancient forms of society, debts represented the very basis of social ties, rather than a superimposed structure of economic domination.[7] Indeed, it has been shown that debts produce and reproduce the social world as such. Reciprocal obligations, mutual provisions and ritualized expenditures are said in societies not defined by a state or a market to play key roles in conflict avoidance, mutual recognition, the sharing of social responsibilities and authority, or the granting of honors.[8] As wealth and sumptuous goods went back and forth, governed by inexplicit albeit generally understood and accepted rules, the individual propensity to conquer and despoil is said to have been tamed where the maintenance of mutual debts bound every member of the community together.[9]

While it may be true, in this sense, that not all use of debt is fundamentally violent and a source of social disintegration, such a caveat has invited some to suggest that there must be a threshold defining acceptable levels of indebtedness or legitimate terms for it.[10] Others have argued, likewise, that if properly maintained and nourished, the mutual dependence represented by indebtedness could, from such a perspective, restore social ties and promote healthier social forms.[11] According to some critiques of the debt economy, reciprocity is offered as the genuine *interest* rooting all social ties. Therefore, arguments have been made that it takes a very narrow understanding of "interest" to refer it exclusively to the financial incentive driving money lenders today. Hence the proposal that we reframe the conversation about economic obligations in terms of what we all owe one another, and what the few owe the many.[12] I would like to engage with and challenge this proposal in order to be clearer about the extent to which we can realistically expect to tackle present-day practices of the "debt economy"[13] by way of such an alternative notion of interest.

The blind spot of the reciprocity hypotheses

It seems that while the social structures of indebtedness may be diverse and liable to produce a variety of outcomes, all practical arrangements available to sociological inquiry share a common feature. All debt systems have the same anthropological ground, whereby debt is created out of the fear or hatred for the individual appetites that would take whatever is desired without, in return, offering just compensation.[14] Imaginations of a more altruistic or mutual indebtedness do not escape this rule (perhaps even a law?), and therefore, although they intend to, they may not yield altogether different economic structures. Exemplified by gift and counter-gift exchanges, the obligation to pay back everything one dares to take tames possible antisocial desires and represents the most efficient tool for securing obedience.[15] Friedrich Nietzsche, for one, reads the very process of civilization in this way. For the German philosopher, to become human means precisely to become "an animal [having] *the right to make promises*." He explains that "Man himself must first of all have become *calculable, regular*, necessary...if he is to be able to stand security for *his own future*."[16] A human being is an animal that is rendered able to comply with his commitments and, so, to pay his debts. Debt tames. It tempers. It domesticates the savage drives and, in so doing, it marks the social body with the seal of "necessity, regularity, calculability." Debt reveals the economy of force required by anthropological becoming.

No matter what the arrangement, debt provides for a power system to ensure its own reproduction. For Georges Bataille, this is also not specific to the recent regime of accumulation. All historical forms of sovereignty, he insists, have rested on the irrational subordination of an "accursed share" or a remainder of energy that, according to the rules of an "economy on a universal scale," must be liberated, used up or sacrificed.[17] As the pivot of an historical extraction process, the present-day debt system is the sort of technology that impedes the proper discharge of such a "share," and it is not so different from what has prevailed in previous historical formations.

One could lament that present-day debt economies enable and perhaps refine relationships of power, but doing so does not much improve our analysis, as it mostly just reasserts the truth that domination is exerted through indebtedness and obfuscates the very motives that create debt in the first place. Instead, when looked at from the perspective of the general economy, processes of indebtedness reveal an irrational and subordinate waste. Such a waste is *uneconomical*. Far from indebtedness being only evidence of social decay, therefore, its particular features serve as indicators of those specific structures of interest that animate each historical formation and which can be described as "hostile to life." Indeed, it is worth pondering whether those sketches of alternative patterns of indebtedness proposed by myriad attempts to politicize the condition of being in debt remain, hopelessly, trapped by the logic of the "restrictive economy," wherein one can only govern the pursuit of a system's growth and the creation of greater units of domination. In this way I hope to help reveal some of the consequences of such "limiting" ways of thinking.

Debt as inscription

Implying that indebtedness is an undesirable and perhaps

shameful situation, Adam Smith once asked, "What can be added to a man who is in health, is out of debt and has a clear conscience?"[18] Clearly, creditor-debtor relationships have, since early modern times, been characterized by a rationalized legal and judicial apparatus meant to ensure that all financial obligations are duly executed, even in cases where it seems humanly impossible to oblige. Moreover, in order to reinforce such legal apparatuses, numerous discursive and ideological constructions have depicted indebtedness as the result, exclusively, of an individual's own moral failures. States that are unable to meet their financial obligations are looked upon as villains, and individuals who default on their debt obligations are considered to be living irresponsibly.[19]

However, according to sociological and anthropological research into the gift and the economy, such moralizing about indebtedness is only a relatively recent state of affairs. Our current and very narrow financial understanding of debt does not exhaust its sociological and anthropological significance. Before it came to refer to a strictly financial relationship, debt played a key role in many religious and ethical belief systems, serving as a method of addressing conflicts and promoting social cohesion. It is only recently, in the course of modern history, that the significance of debt has been narrowed to nothing more than a financial obligation.[20]

Pondering this now hegemonic narrative about indebtedness, some have come to doubt the validity of the specifically economic conceptions of credit, namely, the hypothesis derived by eighteenth-century economists about the bartering of first peoples and the primacy of acquisition-oriented activities. Marcel Mauss and Karl Polanyi, for example, have demonstrated that it is the gift and the counter-gift of symbolic objects, rather than the fair exchange of necessary goods, that represents the fundamental motivation for social interactions; in other words, that debt precedes exchange. Debt is not, as modern economists since Adam Smith have claimed, an exchange awaiting settlement. Such is the thesis of David Graeber's *Debt: the First 5000 Years*, which gathers a tremendous number of examples of highly sophisticated social practices that sustain and nourish social bonds through mutual obligations.[21] Thus, Graeber suggests that Adam Smith's view is rather short-sighted. In the light of such an analysis, the social world appears as the constant circulation of goods rather than an economy based on the satisfaction of needs and the principle of equivalence.

Ritual gift is further analyzed as the most ancient basis for negotiating contacts, initiating intercourse and sealing alliances. One gives in order to risk a relationship; while the counterpart acknowledges the gift by giving back.[22] These structures have even left traces throughout Indo-European languages. According to French linguist Émile Benveniste, the Latin *hostis* refers to those who have exchanged such goods or honors, and who, therefore, owe each other "hospitality."[23] This mutual obligation does not make them friends or equals, though it does establish practices, develop mores and determine what honors ought to be granted to whom. Such is the purpose of indebtedness, to create distinctions and sustain patterns of authority. In other words, debt serves the purpose of *marking*, in the sense of circumscribing or tracing, the *socius*.

Frédéric Lordon's Spinozist form of economic anthropology confirms this hypothesis about the primacy and productivity of debt. He contends that French sociology has put too much emphasis on "giving," whereas it is the "taking" that provoked the most serious anxieties in early social formations.[24] When properly examined, the social concern for the obligation to receive what is given betrays an anguish about the antisocial and unilateral *taking*. In gift economies, the possibility that one might destroy the conditions for the very existence of the group is averted by the rule governing how one can only take that which has been given, and by the codes of honor imposing that one accept a gift and give in turn. Such a relationship, as Lordon has demonstrated, is a sublimation of that fundamental drive to get a hold of everything individual desires invest.[25] Thus, as Pierre Bourdieu has also demonstrated, a gift always conceals the possibility of enslavement.[26] In light of this analysis, to "give" begins to appear less a precondition for moral bonds than a mode of political subjection to hierarchical structures.

Indeed, if debt is understood as a political technology designed to subject, or to mark, as in to outline or characterize the social body, what can be observed here is a continuity, rather than a rupture, between gift and market economies, regardless of how the authority of each is organized around different principles. In a market economy, while the modalities of provision and settlement are governed ostensibly by the principle of objectivity and equivalence, the so-called spontaneity of such arrangements is misleading.

As Graeber has extensively demonstrated, economic analyses of credit often commit the mistake of relying on an assumption that has never been proven accurate, namely that exchanges are driven by the logic of self-sustenance. Likewise, I would suggest that we fall into the same trap whenever we look at debt as an unjust situation and therefore feel indignant. For now, though, suffice it to remark that the idea of the primacy of self-sustenance, which is to say that anything one acquires compensates directly for the loss of something of equivalent value, cannot be attached to any known historical formation with the possible and striking exception of the period between the beginning of the nineteenth and the second half of the twentieth centuries. This is the only episode in world history where such an economic "law" can be said to apply – an era in which markets were flourishing, the gold standard provided some stability and confidence to investors, and liquid assets allowed for wages to be paid on time. During that relatively short historical window, debt was actually an anomaly and indebtedness could meaningfully be framed as a sort of shame.[27]

Michel Aglietta refers, though, to that era as the realization of an "intellectual project" based on the exploitation of proletarian labor and responding expressly to the needs and pressures felt by the *bourgeois* mode of appropriation.[28] This historical formation required imagining that agents in market relationships give *each other* money, which then functions as a neutral instrument aiming to facilitate transactions. We owe this ideological development to John Locke, who contends that "the invention of money, and the tacit agreement of men to put a value on it, introduced (by consent) larger possessions and a right to them."[29] Hence, money is considered as a naturally given, if transitory, repository of the value of things and is not, as such, deemed contingent upon any preexisting social or political relationships. However, many anthropologists have argued that the invention of money cannot be separated from its role in relationships of command and obedience, or in the distribution of privilege and the power to control other people's fate. In short, money cannot be considered except in relation to indebtedness,[30] and its anomalous nature, described above, is nothing but fiction.

Similarly, it is important to note that, while all money is tied to some form of debt, all debts do not necessarily have a monetary equivalent. Thus, Graeber recalls that many credit mechanisms, such as tabs and expense accounts, existed long before cash itself. Money would be pointless in a society shaped by constant reminders about how generations of our ancestors have been sharing, or where institutions remain "to stop lenders from teaming up with bureaucrats and politicians to squeeze everybody dry, as they seem to be doing now."[31] As Graeber has argued, in order to be able to impose the law of value and to numerically specify the exact amount due, one must be on the side of the powerful.[32] A creditor must beforehand possess a certain degree of technical and economic superiority to be able to take what is *owed* according to the principles of objectivity and equivalence. Thus, legal forms of credit might, in this sense, represent the ultimate refinement of that "taking" drive that underlies all social formations. If debt, in all its historical configurations, amounts to the social inscription of a system of power, the point here would be to provide a clear account of the ways it operates in our own specific contexts; which is to say that, if debt is a means of writing the social into being, what, exactly, do current regimes of indebtedness have to say about us now?

Power and accumulation

"Primitive accumulation" is the expression used by Marx to describe the precondition of capitalist modes of production, namely the violent methods used in the process of separating the workers from their means of production. Among such methods was the "enclosure of common pastures";[33] although indebtedness has also represented a powerful means of dispossessing people of the means of their own subsistence, and not necessarily in the manner one would think. Graeber, for example, argues simultaneously that debt is the mechanism through which the immediate ownership of the means of production is destroyed, and that the decisive task of "primitive accumulation" is accomplished, paradoxically, through the *criminalization* of indebtedness. Thus, alongside the dismantling of peasant societies, the systems formerly used to protect debtors were also done away with. Personal agreements, tabs and expense accounts, for example, all were made illegal as cash payment was imposed and supported by a corresponding arsenal of legal and judicial resources.

Arguably, when looking at modern political and economic structures, the purpose of debt seems to be only to despoil, extort and subjugate, which is very different from confirming reciprocal obligations that, through our giving and returning, bind us otherwise to one another. It may not be accurate that all debts are mere instruments used by a hegemonic class to establish and reinforce its own exclusive dominion, but it can be argued that debts, more generally, *create* and *maintain* certain structures of power. Domination is the result, then, not the cause, of indebtedness. In fact, in all of its different arrangements, debt functions as an "inscription"; the social body being fashioned through some specific articulation or marking of the fundamental bonds of indebtedness. While the distinctive features of traditional gift and contemporary market economies may seem evident, one should also observe the common motive behind all such historical formations. The material forces underlying our own formation, for instance, can now be highlighted.

In *The Genealogy of Morals*, Nietzsche also insists on the economic motivation of legal norms. Indeed, any technology ensuring that every single act of appropriation entails both an actor and some opposing party can be understood as producing a specific anthropological formation and, as such, every accumulation of forces reveals, from the perspective of the general economy, a properly *uneconomical* or irrational and detrimental waste of energy. The legal means that govern the settlement of economic obligations are the source of a not insignificant expense that serves the concentration of power and of all means of exertion. Nietzsche, in this sense, proposed an evaluation of "the oldest and naivest moral canon of *justice*," which he finds in the principle according to which "everything has its price, and all things can be paid for."[34] As such, this original and most elemental moral code was inherited from the most elementary of social complexes. It is only much later that the need for law was actually felt, for when constant resistance opposes the imposition of will and power, then the primitive moral canon of justice must yield to a permanent institution. The economy of this concretion is as follows: having to constantly tackle *reactive* forces, the most powerful imagine a technology capable of definitively suppressing such expressions of what Nietzsche called *ressentiment*. The discontent of those who suffer the savage appropriation of potent individuals would otherwise mobilize most part of their vital energy. Nietzsche, of course, does not celebrate such an antisocial force, but ponders instead the consequence of such dynamics on the *quality* of the will. Here is the evaluation he proposes:

> From the highest biological standpoint, legal conditions can never be other than *exceptional conditions*, since they constitute a partial restriction of the will of life, which is bent upon power, and are subordinate to its total goal as a single means: namely, as a means of creating greater units of power.[35]

A state is required when prominent individuals feel so threatened by the reaction they arouse that they need to prevent accounts being left open and debts left to run. Power becomes so precarious that it feels the need to constantly reassert its mastery, and the greater the "unit of that power" in question, the greater the demand for repression in turn. At an advanced level of specialization, the operator of such social control can no longer simply be honor and moral authority. Thus, an impersonal and objective form of justice is instantiated by a legal framework and enacted by the appropriate repressive organization; objectivity and justice are the marks left by the writing of that concretion of power.

Such a dynamic expresses how, just as the ritual gift is a technology that enables the preservation of power, the rules of economic exchange are part of a technology of accumulation. The same sublimation of the will to take for oneself anything one desires is the very core of anthropological production, that becoming human. Nietzsche describes the economy of such complexities as follows:

> A legal order thought of as sovereign and universal, not as a means in the struggle between power complexes but

as a means of *preventing* all struggle in general [...] would be a principle *hostile to life*, an agent of the dissolution and destruction of man, an attempt to assassinate the future of man, a sign of weariness, a secret path to nothingness.[36]

Thus, we might say that the supreme power of appropriation – the state and the notion of private property – can only rule at the expense of taming and subjugating *all* individual desires. A dominion that pursues its objectives under the guise of a "sovereign and universal legal order" is liable to rule through systematic despoilment, which is, as Nietzsche puts it, a "principle *hostile to life*," and particularly the life of those who seem to most benefit from such dominion. Indeed, this is the very definition of *uneconomical*.

In order to get a more concrete understanding of the tendency that Nietzsche is attempting to name, it is interesting to recall that at some precise point in history, recorded even by the history of languages, the mutual hospitality previously encompassed by the term *hostis* vanished and was replaced by more formal and impersonal political entities. When large political and economic structures such as the empire were made to govern the relationships between all city-states and tribes, the *hostis* came to refer only to the foreign and *hostile* other.[37] Instead of representing a more "economical" way of mediating relationships, the formation of "greater units of power" came to represent a systematic endeavor to repress and subdue competing wills, and generally to demean life in the process. Indeed, a formidable expenditure is required to sustain and feed such a concretion of forces; its inscription technology being the least "economical."

Utility and the hypothesis of scarcity

Although historically distinct, principles underlying the gift and the market have organized the obligation to give back in quite similar fashions, and this similarity is due to both having been built upon the same structure of interest. Now, if we hope to get beyond the structural domination of present-day industries of indebtedness, we have to investigate the basis upon which an alternative notion of interest might be founded. Tracing the relationship between such basic economic concepts as the law of value and the notion of utility, one assesses whether the interest in a so-called mutual debt actually stems (or not) from an alternative source.

It would be problematic if, in order to distinguish good debts from bad, one proposed a normative framework that would rely on the concepts of value and utility as such. Intended to avoid the negative consequence of a conception of debt as primitive accumulation, such a method would lead us into the same trap that John Locke fell into when he considered human beings to be, by natural law, first and foremost concerned with utility. It would be tantamount to claiming, as Locke did, that self-sustenance is the fundamental human incentive and that "use value" is an inherent quality of things.

It has become commonplace to scorn such "Utilitarian" politics, but how ready are we really to do away with the search for "usefulness?" To refer to "use value" in order to define an acceptable and legitimate level of indebtedness is indeed to borrow a conceptual framework from the eighteenth-century's political economy, one based on the premise that human societies have always puzzled over, and all practical activities been motivated by, not dissipation but acquisition. While regarding expenditure negatively as the sin of a decadent nobility, modern civil society has shown itself capable of a tremendous increase in the production of wealth. Hypothesizing scarcity, the eighteenth-century economists thought it expedient to make surplus production a condition for the satisfaction of needs, and, consequently, to turn all surplus – now recast as Capital – into a means of "improving" the fruitfulness of economic enterprise.

The expansion of this economic model has made it obvious that capitalistic enterprise, in the end, is but the pursuit of profit for profit's sake. Production and exchange are a means of fulfilling an individual's needs only insofar as such fulfillment is part of an accumulative process. Thus, as Elettra Stimilli has claimed, drawing on Max Weber, production is an "autotelic activity" with no external purpose; a kind of *praxis*.[38] The most significant feature of capitalist production, in this sense, is its *"ascesis"*; the fact that it simply does not allow for or enable expenditure. The concern for usefulness has justified such *ascesis*.

As Richard Dienst once wrote, commenting on a statement Jean-Paul Sartre had made about revolution: "We owe it to ourselves to build" a "dependence on each other."[39] This proposal is worth examining. However, when proposing a "politics of indebtedness," in this way, jettisoning those debts that "deter us from living" and promoting genuine sources of freedom and conditions for healthier social bonds, are we really departing from that misconception that economists had, busy as they were with the acquisition "problem"? Are we not just decrying that capitalism has failed to meet the most basic of human needs for sustenance, all the while referring to that same "utility" that was invented by those who, because they had to sustain a "great unit of power," refused the possibility of gratuitous and irrational waste – like Locke, who found the possibility of uncultivated land to be utterly unbearable?

Is the idea of "collective self-reliance", or of alternative patterns of distribution based on the "obligations that everyone owes,"[40] altogether distinct from Locke's concern with the system of needs? Such alternative projects obviously pursue radically different endeavors, but how liable are they to actually sketch any *economical* solution to the current "crisis"? By "economical," here, I refer to the perspective of a general economy, one that takes into account not just acquisition but also the discharge of the total energy available on the planet. A solution is required, therefore, that would not merely alleviate the "sacrifice" currently made in the name of needs and the logic of interests requiring growth, but would admit too that there is plenty for everyone to use consciously and sacrifice willingly. The purpose is not satisfaction, but the very expression of life, which is expenditure and the opposite of "waste."

In no society have productive activities ever been about self-sustenance. This is why contemporary debt structures cannot be adequately challenged with the notion of "interest" that is entangled with the concept of "value." The reason is that there simply exists no such concept outside those "uneconomical" units of domination already described. In other words, value is created, enhanced and nourished only in the context of a restrictive economy, one that accompanies the reproduction of a system of power. Precisely, it is debt structures that determine value, not some perverse inversion of a natural or immediate quality in things. The realm of "value" is from the outset the realm of historical sovereignty.

According to Bataille's general economy, the purpose of all earthly activities is expressed as surplus production and unproductive consumption. There is a "share," he states, that is exhausted for no useful purpose. The problem is that this *exceeding* part of the energy available on the planet tends to be used to fuel the accumulation of power.[41] Such a failure to consciously discharge that surplus results in a historical formation which, as we learned from Nietzsche, is "hostile to life." Admittedly, referring to the principle of utility in order to define an alternative notion of interest to be used in the framing of political protest against the contemporary debt system can yield a certain redistribution of power. Politicizing the notions of utility and interest can serve as a powerful instrument in the negotiation of privileges and obligations. However, the principle of utility remains dependent upon the "unit of domination" it stems from, even where the domination becomes impersonal and is contained within a legal framework. Utility cannot be considered an economical principle, for it remains intimately tied to the concept of value, a concept belonging to the restrictive economy. As Bataille insists:

> An immense industrial network cannot be managed in the same way that one changes a tire...It [general economy] expresses a circuit of cosmic energy on which it depends, which cannot limit, and whose laws it cannot ignore without consequences. Woe to those who, to the very end, insist on regulating the movement that exceeds them with the narrow mind of the mechanic who changes a tire.[42]

There is *no* science of the human needs, no ideal contribution-provision balance, for human beings are "ontologically marked by a constitutive excess, and their actions cannot be reduced to the productive activities of their self-sustenance."[43] As Bataille admits, the perspective of the general economy raises numerous problems on a practical level, but its interest is unquestionable.[44] Indeed, evaluating the level of irrational expense allows us to address the intricate reality of debt in contemporary capitalism as a warning about the possible consequences of using concepts, like value and utility, that are imbued with *uneconomical* principles. To apply a notion of usefulness belonging to a restrictive economy may lead to a social power that generalizes and equalizes the sacrifice thought of as the condition of self-sustenance and may not allow us to see that free dissipation is, indeed, the very process of life. Sacrifice is a praxis, not a means to an end.

Speculative conclusion

The perspective of a general economy offers a fresh gaze upon the issues raised by the actual politics of debt. As such, it yields a critical assessment of an anthropological formation that demands the sacrifice of life. There is no either-or alternative here, but one can reflect upon what is renounced when the notions and ideals that were born and fostered in this process of power accumulation are embraced. How has it been established that the possibility that one takes anything without owing afterwards appears to be fundamentally violent and a source of social disintegration? From a Spinozist point of view, Lordon suggests, taking appears as the expression of that endeavor of every living being to persist in being.[45] The "will to life itself" takes freely and dissipates for the sole celebration of its own existence. But what exactly does such "will to life" take and dissipate? What is profitable to such a savage will? One cannot say. Asking the question, though, allows us to see that the claim of material wealth or the control of productive forces is the very definition of "profitable" to a certain mode of individuation. The problem, then, is not that one may take for oneself whatever one's desire invests, but indeed the investing of desire in the naturally expansive individual-proprietor described by modern anthropology from Hobbes to Locke.

In order to challenge the social structures of indebtedness, and more specifically those that have been determined by a possessive individualism, it seems pointless, in light of general economy, to imagine a more generous human nature or to reestablish a propensity toward the solidarity of exchange. As Mauss stated: "The ideal would be to give a potlatch that is not returned."[46] But to give, he knows better than anybody else, is always to hope to get something in return, always some refinement of taking, and not necessarily less brutal than it is to sell according to market rules. There must exist a manner of giving such that what is expected "in return" is not the obedience and subjugation of the receiver, but the very existence of *another power complex*, namely, the receiver, him or herself. Such co-presence and rivalry may, indeed, reveal itself to be profitable, however in a manner altogether different.

2. Credit as Political Technology

Jean-François Bissonnette
Université de Montréal

In Shakespeare's *Hamlet*, published in 1603, old Polonius gives his son Laertes a piece of advice that strangely resonates with the situation of millions today: "Neither a borrower nor a lender be, for loan oft loses both itself and friend, and borrowing dulls the edge of husbandry." This is quite a strong warning against debt, and yet there is something rather quaint about it. To be sure, lending is not as risky and friendless as it used to be. Lenders have powerful friends in high places who bail them out whenever they stand to lose their money. Borrowing, on the other hand, isn't so bad either, apparently. On the contrary, if you read financial advice literature, it is rather presented as a sign of "good" husbandry. Indeed, to borrow is to grow, as they say.

Whereas Shakespeare wrote nearly one century before the start of what historians call the British "financial revolution," we now live in a fully-fledged form of capitalism in which finance dominates and permeates every layer of social life. One expression of this financialization of society is the development of a phenomenon I would describe as a "culture of indebtedness." People throughout the developed world are going deeper and deeper into debt. The growth in household debt over the last 20 to 30 years has been staggering. For instance, in the Netherlands, average household debt increased from 148 percent of net disposable income in 1995, to 276 percent in 2015, according to the OECD.[1] In Canada, over the same period, household debt jumped from 103 percent to 175 percent. In Australia, it more than doubled to reach 211 percent. In the United Kingdom, it grew from 102 percent to 149 percent, after having peaked at 173 percent in 2007. Americans also started deleveraging following the 2008 crisis, bringing their overall debt down 32 percent from its 143 percent peak at the start of the crash, but after nearly a decade on the decrease, it is now rising again both in Britain and the US.

We know that the 2007-2008 financial crash was triggered by the American subprime mortgage market going haywire. Perhaps some started heeding Polonius' advice and reduced their exposure afterwards, but as a whole, a striking fact remains: debt has been completely normalized in the contemporary economic culture. Being in debt is now part of a patently normal way of life. And as it happens, this cultural normalization of debt over the last 2 or 3 decades coincided with the entrenchment of neoliberalism in the developed world. Most economists would probably say that rising debt is merely an effect of the law of supply and demand, mirroring the increased value of assets, particularly on the real estate market. But is there not a political aspect to this phenomenon of ballooning private debt? How can we understand it, and how does it participate in defining who we are as individuals in the neoliberal era?

Debt and the collapse of social democracy

To explain this phenomenon, one perspective would consist in analyzing the transformation of economic policy, broadly understood as a shift from social democracy to neoliberalism, which is arguably a reflection of conflicting class interests. Wolfgang Streeck makes this kind of argument in his book *Buying Time*.[2] Streeck claims that the rise in private debt today is largely a result of states attempting to consolidate their budgets. Austerity, in other words, would amount to a privatization of the public debt. Governments would simply shift the debt burden onto individuals, and this would signal a dramatic shift in class relationships.

Streeck here follows an argument put forth by Colin Crouch,

who claims that the current economic policy regime is better understood as a form of "privatized Keynesianism."[3] Whereas classical Keynesianism advocated a strategic use of public debt to stabilize the economy and provide social security to populations, slashing public budgets in the name of financial responsibility would now force these populations to use credit as a means to ensure their own security and well-being.

Streeck adds to this argument by saying that the public debt that is now being privatized was itself the result of the collapse of the class compromise that sustained social democracy. The welfare state was meant to secure the allegiance of workers to the capitalist system, by providing them with a social safety net that compensated for their exploitation while perpetuating it for the benefit of capital owners. High taxes were the price to pay for this compromise to work. At some point during the 1960s and 70s, however, the wealthy had had enough, and they either managed to convince governments to lower tax rates, or found new ways to avoid paying taxes altogether. Confronted with declining tax revenues, states thus had to borrow massively in order to maintain public services and benefits that their populations held dear. By the same token, mounting public debt offered the propertied class with a secure and profitable investment opportunity in the form of government bonds. Tax evaders became debt collectors of sorts.

Public debt and private debt would thus form the two pillars of a system of class domination. There are some who go so far as to say that we no longer live in a democracy, but in a "creditocracy," as Andrew Ross calls it.[4] Creditors would form a social class that dominates society; making sure, on the one hand, that government priorities align with the consolidation and repayment of the public debt owed to them, while feeding on ordinary citizens, on the other hand, by forcing them into a debt trap and making them pay interests in perpetuity, now that it has become nearly impossible to live one's life and satisfy one's basic needs without using credit.

Although I think that such a class analysis of economic policy is necessary, and that it is indeed crucial to understand debt as a form of exploitation, it is nevertheless reductive in my view to consider the growth in private debt as merely a result of the functional needs of the class struggle, rendered manifest, as it were, through the contradictions of fiscal and budgetary policy. I would like for my part to try and describe the increase in private debt in a different light, by analyzing it not only as an effect but as the very instrument of a specific form of political rationality, which consists in the radical extension of the market logic within both state institutions and society. This program relies on a definite remolding of subjectivity, which consists in transforming citizens into "leveraged speculators." Credit and debt can be conceived of in this regard as a typically neoliberal example of what Michel Foucault called a "political technology of individuals," that is, as an instrument that serves a "technical project" that aims to establish a "correlation between the utility scale for individuals and the utility scale for the state."[5] In other words, to attain certain political objectives, the state has to take into account, influence and instrumentalize the ways in which individuals perceive and act in their self-interest.

Credit is such a political technology, and it played an instrumental role in neoliberalism's attempt to remodel society in its own image. What I would like to show is that by incentivizing individuals to take on debt as a means of accessing certain goods and opportunities, neoliberal governments actually sought to introduce and ingrain the market logic within the social realm. In other words, their "technical project" consists in altering the "utility scale for individuals" in order to make debt appear useful and profitable, so as to boost the utility scale for the state, insofar as the latter is now coextensive with the performance of the market. Two examples of this come to mind: mortgage debt and student debt.

Dwelling in debt

Encouraging homeownership has been a key feature of the neoliberal agenda since the 1980s. In the United Kingdom, for instance, it was a flagship measure of Margaret Thatcher's tenure as prime minister. Her idea was to create a so-called "ownership society." As Thatcher said: "where property is widely owned, freedom flourishes."[6] At the time, Britain had the largest pool of social housing in Western Europe. In order to "liberate" people from this "collectivist trap" and establish a "property-owning democracy," her government set out to privatize these immense assets by offering tenants the "right to buy" their flat. The basic idea was thus that the state should stop catering to people's needs. Instead, it should incentivize them to start accumulating assets, that is, it should transform tenants into investors. Property means freedom and freedom means responsibility, so let people take their chance on the market, reap the benefits and assume the risks.

Of course, to be able to exercise their "right to buy," people had to borrow money. Liberalizing the financial sector, which was another central element of the neoliberal agenda, conveniently made sure that people would have access to a never-ending flow of credit. By making prospective homeowners tap into these world-spanning financial flows, domestic everyday life thus became entangled in unprecedented ways with global economic structures, whose growth depended in turn on the former's desire to buy a home and willingness to borrow.

In the process, the very meaning of "home" would change. "Home" is now a synonym for financial asset. As Manuel Aalbers writes, "the financialization of home forces more and more households to see acquiring a house not just as a home, as a place to live, but as an investment, as something to put equity into and take equity from."[7] What matters most in this peculiar conception of domesticity is no longer the material security that the home provides, but the potential capital gain that its future sale promises. Contracting a mortgage and buying a house are punctual decisions that partake in a life-long strategy, which is, for some people at least, to climb the "property ladder" in a never-ending project of capital accumulation.[8]

Debt is but a means to that end. In the jargon of finance, this is called "leverage": using debt as a speculative instrument in order to maximize future returns. Leverage indeed allows investors to amplify their gains by borrowing several times their initial capital, thus increasing the size of their investment and their future profits. Making people desire home ownership[9] and take on significant debts to achieve this goal was thus a crucial instrument in a political strategy that consisted both in freeing the state from its obligation as provider of public services such as subsidized housing, and in reorienting the national economic strategy toward the growth of the financial sector. Unless we think that humans are "naturally" motivated by a possessive and accumulative drive, we have to consider that these desires are socially and politically produced. Reframing property as essential to personal freedom and security, and as a stepping stone to social mobility and asset accumulation contributed to the entrenchment of a "culture of indebtedness." Debt appears as a leveraging tool that supposedly unlocks long-term benefits. In that sense, our culture of indebtedness is indissociable from the growth of a "speculative ethos" at the subjective level.

Learning the meaning of debt

The other example of this speculative use of credit is student debt, which is blowing out of proportion in most English-speaking countries. The UK again offers a clear example of the political rationality behind rising debt, which also consists in correlating individual utility scales and state political objectives. In his 2010 report to the British government[10], which proved influential for the radical reform of the higher education sector that soon followed, Lord Browne proposed deregulating tuition fees as a means of ensuring the global competitiveness of British universities in the so-called "knowledge economy." To perform better, universities needed additional resources. Increasing government funding was ruled out, however, as that was supposedly unfair to the taxpayers who had not themselves benefited from a university education. These additional resources would rather come from the students. By paying higher tuition fees, students were thus to play a strategic role in imposing on universities the market discipline deemed necessary to improve their performance and competitiveness.

The underlying logic was that the benefits of higher education mostly accrue to the private individual, even if a better trained workforce is also essential to the strengthening of the national economy as a whole. Since education is framed in the report as merely a form of professional training, students are thus essentially considered as wage earners in waiting.[11] Their prospects on the job market and their future income depend on the decisions they make upon entering university. Students thus have to choose among competing academic institutions the one that presents the most valuable option, that is, the curriculum that offers the best employment opportunities. In doing so, their choice constitutes a market signal that universities must heed in order to attract the students' money, by improving the "appeal" and "quality" of their educational offer. In order to steer universities toward adopting a market logic, while lowering the cost for the state, this strategy thus relied on students whose rational decision-making was to act as a selection mechanism to distinguish "world class" universities from poorly performing institutions that would soon be obliterated by recurrent underfunding.

For rational decision makers, higher tuition fees had to have a negative effect on their motivation to enroll. Lord Browne insisted, however, that despite its increased cost, a degree was still a "good investment." It is widely believed that university graduates earn a sizable wage "premium" over the length of their working life. One former British education minister even put that figure at no less than £400,000.[12] If students were indeed utility maximizers, the prospect of earning such a premium should easily offset their initial expenditure. Having the possibility to borrow the money needed to study would make their choice easier still, since students would not even need to pay up front. Just like a cunning investor, students could take advantage of the "leverage effect" of borrowing.

Lord Browne's proposals established a finance scheme in which students would start paying their debts only once their income reached a certain level, thus making borrowing supposedly "risk free." Students could hardly refuse such a deal: if they could make a risk-free investment in their own employability now so as to reap immense returns later, the prospect of life-long indebtedness should not be cause for concern. In any case, English students, living in a country where universities were still entirely free 20 years ago, now find themselves the most heavily indebted compared with their peers in other Anglophone countries, where student debt is also on the rise.[13] The political rationality behind the accumulation of student debt worldwide is indeed the same. Now that higher education is conceived of as a financial investment that only benefits the individual, students have to consider themselves as "leveraged investor subjects," as Paul Langley says of homeowners.[14] Students have to speculate on their capacity to convert their degree into a steady stream of income, which obviously depends on the unpredictable economic conjuncture in which they will find themselves upon graduation. Considering the debt load that comes with it, their decision to enroll in university implies calculating the odds that their choice will eventually pay out. Students are being turned into gamblers. Since credit essentially constitutes an advance on future income, their borrowing is but a wager on their future solvency.

Debt, freedom and discipline

If we accept Foucault's idea that neoliberalism urges individuals to become "entrepreneurs of themselves," and to adopt various strategies so as to maximize their own "human capital" and their overall performance in every sphere of life[15], then the contemporary "culture of indebtedness" indicates that the use of credit has come to have precisely this kind of strategic value for the self. As the two examples I discussed show, debt is being used as a speculative tool in a strategy that consists in accumulating material and immaterial assets. And there is no denying that some debtors at least gain considerable advantages thanks to this leverage. Contra Shakespeare, then, it seems that borrowing does not *dull* the edge of husbandry; it *sharpens* it. Borrowers are financially empowered; they borrow so they can grow.

The neoliberal concept of debt is thus quite ambivalent: public debt is bad, it constrains the nation's future and the only answer to that is perpetual austerity. But private debt is good, if used wisely. Debt, it seems, is both an effect and a condition of freedom. People are free to borrow or not, and borrowing is meant to make them even more free. Credit enlarges the array of choices they can make, and gives them access to resources that increase their life chances more generally. What is there to criticize then, if people go into debt willingly, and if debt helps them move forward with their lives?

There has been a certain debate among interpreters regarding what Foucault actually thought of neoliberalism. Some suggest that Foucault might have been seduced by the neoliberal Utopia, that is, before it actually started being implemented.[16] Governing through freedom seemed to harbor the promise of a post-disciplinary politics, one in which individuals would no longer be subjected to the kind of authoritarian "molding" that characterized disciplinary institutions such as the school, the factory, the barracks or the prison, where compliance to a single overarching norm was key.[17] Resonating with the counter-cultural ideals of the 1960s and 70s, neoliberalism offered the possibility for individuals to choose their own norm. Freedom of choice was thus freedom to become who you wanted to be.

"Man is no longer man enclosed, but man in debt," remarked Gilles Deleuze.[18] Indeed, as I argued here, our contemporary culture of indebtedness echoes the libertarian promise that made neoliberalism so alluring. Credit is but a tool that facilitates the exercise of freedom, a stepping stone with which one can create one's future. This future-orientedness of neoliberal subjectivity is at the heart of a speculative ethos, whereby every decision has to be made according to an anticipation of its future profitability. Such an ethos is crucial to the political rationality of neoliberalism. The "utility scale for the state," which consists in reducing its commitments to society as a service and benefits provider, while ensuring the growth of the economy and the penetration of the market logic into society, depends on the "utility scale for individuals," and on their readiness to take on debt to finance their expenditures and notably to access goods and services that the state used to provide in the heyday of social democracy. Reframing debt as a form of economic empowerment is crucial to cultivating this subjective disposition and to make the entire arrangement seem acceptable.

Important as it seems for a political rationality that aims to govern society through individual freedom, debt remains, however, a type of power relationship that relies heavily on discipline. Debt is indeed a promise to pay back. This is the moral underbelly of financialized capitalism. Yet, if credit literally means "faith," simple trust is not enough for it to function properly. The global financial system thus depends on the functioning of a gigantic surveillance apparatus in order to supplement the "payback morality"[19] of credit and to enforce financial self-discipline on the part of indebted subjects, so that their behavior aligns with the imperative of debt repayment.

This largely private surveillance complex, which mainly functions through proprietary credit-scoring and transaction-tracking algorithmic technologies, now spans the whole social fabric, monitoring everyone's behavior and classifying every individual according to their capacity or willingness to pay their debts.[20] Such classifications can have far-reaching consequences that stretch well beyond the capacity to obtain a loan. In the United States, notably, it is common for employers or landlords to ask for the credit score of their would-be employees or tenants, as if this score was a reliable measure of one's character. In neoliberal societies, personal life chances thus largely depend on one's compliance with the normative expectations of the financial industry. Maintaining a good credit score is thus crucial to the extent that being "free" depends on one's capacity to access certain goods and accumulate certain assets. While this presupposes an engagement in consumerist behavior, it also requires discipline and self-restraint, as if one had to internalize the all-seeing gaze of the financial industry.

Debt as a form of disciplinary power thus appears as a formidable tool of capitalist exploitation. Returning to the first perspective sketched out at the beginning of this chapter, that of class relations, it appears that the rise of private debt is not only a result of the demise of the political compromise of social democracy, but the sign of a new stage in the historical class struggle within capitalism. In its classical, Marxist sense, exploitation took place on the factory floor. Workers had no choice to survive but to sell their labor and let their employers profit from their work. I would argue that debt now stretches the domain of exploitation beyond work to encompass spheres of life, such as home-dwelling and studying, that are not productive per se, but which it turns into additional sources of profit, through the magic of compound interests. I would add that debt also contributes to the exploitation of workers by making them more docile and disciplined, since they depend so much on their wages to be able to pay back their debts.

And yet, people embrace debt as a useful tool and for apparently good reason: owning their home or having a university degree often makes them better off, after all. Is it not paradoxical? And if there is indeed an exploitative aspect to debt, what is it? Self-exploitation? "Voluntary servitude?" Perhaps neoliberalism gives us renewed reason to read La Boétie.

3. Debt and Utopia

Richard Dienst
Rutgers University

Debt and Utopia? There must be some mistake. Surely all of us associate debt with dystopia, with dysfunctional economies, dead-end societies and blocked lives. The breakdown of the social safety net drives people into personal debt as soon as they cannot afford to buy food, or receive health care, or pay for school, or find a place to live. Consumer debt invites everyone to participate in the so-called abundance of our age, necessities and luxuries alike, but only if their credit score is high enough. Corporate debt spreads speculative risks throughout the economy, not least through the opaque dealings of the financial sector. And public debt continues to erode the prospects for democratic sovereignty, discounting the common good according to the priorities and prerogatives of central bankers and bond traders. To be permanently in debt – everyday life as a combination of voluntary servitude and collective doom – seems like a basic feature of any dystopia, especially the one we are living through right now.

So it might seem that the only Utopian response to the system of debt is to escape it. And yet recent history shows us that that is not so easy. There are four basic ways to do it: 1) to pay off your debts, 2) to refuse to pay them, 3) to be forgiven, or 4) to defer payment until the debts have lost their value. All of these maneuvers involve some kind of negotiation with the institutions that police credit, and so none of them actually challenge the system of debts itself. As the experience of Strike Debt has shown, it has proven difficult to aggregate acts of defiance and default into a political force. Must Utopia go further, then: not just to erase or escape the debts we have, but to break the economic and legal apparatuses that create debt, in order to ensure that nobody will need to go into debt ever again? Can we even imagine such a society? Is that really what we want?

What can we hope for?

Here I am not going to offer a Utopian blueprint for remaking the debt economy. That's not to say that it cannot be done. Instead I want to invoke Utopia as a method, in the sense developed by Fredric Jameson. Of course, the modern understanding of Utopian thinking is grounded in the monumental work of Ernst Bloch, especially his three-volume *Das Prinzip Hoffnung* (The Principle of Hope), written over the course of several decades and originally published by Suhrkamp in 1959. Bloch was introduced to English-language critics by Jameson, who devoted a key chapter of his 1971 book *Marxism and Form* to Bloch, and who has continued to write about Utopia all the way up to his recent works, *Archaeologies of the Future: Utopia and Other Science Fictions* (2005) and *An American Utopia: Dual Power and the Universal Army* (2016). I'll come back to the latter book at the end, but for now I want to outline a basic distinction about this approach to Utopian thinking: the difference between Utopian programs and Utopian impulses.

From Thomas More onward, Utopian *programs* have been provocations to the imagination. A program, like a manifesto, is a text that announces a break and outlines something new. In all the disputations that follow, the audience is invited to make all of the usual objections: to say why there can be nothing new, why it will never work, why nothing ever changes for the better, but always for the worse. In the face of such reflexes, grappling with a Utopian program is a very good exercise in learning about the limits of what we allow ourselves to think: how far we can experimentally break away from our usual sense of what is possible, and how far we even want to try. In English, there is a great idiom for this process: to "entertain a thought," which means that we can consider a thought without committing to it, which yields a bonus of pleasure in the process. For many of us, perhaps, literary texts and artworks offer the best opportunities to entertain thoughts; indeed, as Thoreau once said, "all matter, indeed, is capable of entertaining thought" – a splendid maxim for Utopians.[1] For while Utopian programs posit a certain kind of rupture and closure, we only ever access such thoughts by way of imaginative leaps and provisional speculations.

The Utopian *impulse* is something rather different. In order to see it, we must adopt a strong hermeneutic hypothesis: that human beings pursue their activities through a future-oriented drive. That is to say, we need to develop the interpretive skills to detect Utopian impulses in all kinds of texts and situations, even dystopian ones, in order to show how wishes disguise themselves in order to keep their chances alive. Although Bloch calls this force "hope," it can be closely aligned with the fundamental forces named in other theoretical systems, including conatus in Spinoza and Eigensinn in Negt and Kluge. Taken on this scale, Bloch's hypothesis would be as far-reaching as Freud's positing of the unconscious, to which it bears a certain resemblance, although it breaks decisively from Freud's fundamental orientation toward the past, the frustrations of memory and the exhausting inertia of death within which the psychoanalytic system works. As Jameson puts it: "the Freudian unconscious is a no-longer-consciousness," while Bloch proposes "a very different type of unconscious," a "not-yet–consciousness."[2]

In yet another sense, the "Utopian impulse" begins to resemble the notion of "desire" in its most expansive forms. Here the emphasis falls on three key features: its orientation to anticipation rather than memory; its inner and outer collective dimensions; and its fundamental difference and distance from "what is." To the degree that the Utopian impulse or desire pursues fulfillment by negating the present, we might recoil from its apparently exorbitant demands; if so, we then have to ask ourselves how far our ordinary, "responsible" tastes and preferences mark a fatal compromise with an inevitably faulty picture of the present, and therefore lead to a weakening of our ability to make a better life for ourselves and others.

According to Jameson's reading of Bloch, then, we can trace a tradition of Utopian programs through all of the famous and not-so-famous texts; and at the same time, we can find the Utopian impulse at work everywhere, and not only in places that announce themselves as Utopian. We learn to see how wishes animate all kinds of behavior and projects, from shopping to education, from going to the gym to paying taxes. Indeed, the hermeneutic does not stop there: even obsessive thoughts about death or reactionary political speeches reveal themselves to be caught up with wishes. Thus we come to understand that the reactive or debilitating character of such expressions is due to blocked circumstances and faulty imaginative resources, which can be remedied, rather than to some basic failure of human beings to help themselves. In this interpretive scheme, even the most negative element in our mental and social lives "may therefore serve as a means of access to that positive which it conceals."[3]

Jameson insists that neither of these Utopian tasks can lead to a positive program for a future society or a cure for our inveterate failure to realize our dreams. The point instead is to develop the means to understand the perpetual possibility and historical failure of all Utopian schemes, however clearly articulated or concretely realized. Utopia thus serves as a methodological skyhook or bootstrap for a dialectical deployment of that incessant wishful thinking without which social existence would be impossible.

What do we owe ourselves?

To ask how something like indebtedness might be inscribed in a Utopian conception of social life, I want to offer a somewhat old-fashioned close reading of a phrase made famous by Karl Marx:

From each according to their abilities, to each according to their needs[4]
Jeder nach seinen Fähigkeiten, jedem nach seinen Bedürfnissen

Later I will say a few things about the long history of this phrase, but for now we should ask exactly what kind of a sentence this is. Is it a statement of plain fact? A political proposal? A legal rule? A moral principle? A maxim for everyday life, or an impossible ideal? Can the sentence stand on its own – inscribed on a banner or a bumper sticker – without any further elaboration? Does it strike us as a description of a real, or a good or a true state of affairs?

Note first of all that it does not specify a place or a time for its enactment: more significantly, it does not say whose abilities and needs are being summoned. What kind of group, what kind of timetable and what kind of "us" does it call upon? Does it belong on the wall of a kindergarten? In the vows of a civil union? In the honor code of a soccer league? In the constitution of a state? In a universal declaration of human ideals? Or maybe all of these, and more?

Let us look closely at the relationship between the two phrases. While the back-and-forth grammar leads us to think that they mesh together neatly – as if in an equal exchange or a virtuous circle – we need to ask whether "abilities" and "needs" actually belong to the same semantic register or sphere of practice. Perhaps our abilities and our needs do not really fit together, either at the level of an individual lifetime, or the level of any conceivable social organization, let alone the level of a collective history. While the sentence seems to encourage us to think that these two processes can be coordinated, integrated or balanced, we could just as well begin with the opposite assumption: perhaps "abilities" and "needs" speak different languages, expressing rather different dimensions of experience or existence. Perhaps this Utopian slogan expresses a necessary disarticulation rather than an inevitable equivalence. And, if so, maybe its appeal consists precisely in its promise somehow to cultivate these two otherwise incommensurable dimensions of life: abilities and needs, work and desire, giving and taking, supply and demand, private and public, or what might be called contribution and provision.

Now look at the first part again: "from each according to their abilities." The phrase does not tell us what to do, but only that we must do what we can. The injunction is both general and absolutely particular: everyone must act, but each one will act differently. Strictly speaking, the phrase makes no reference to other people, let alone to a division of labor: we are not asked to "do our fair share," "to do our bit." Instead, the words "from each" inflect mere doing toward doing fully, which may or may not involve "doing more" or "doing differently." As Deleuze says, *To do all we can* is our ethical task properly so called."[5] In the same vein, Brecht's Chinese sage Me-ti says:

> I have not found many "Thou shalt" statements that I have had any desire to propose. I am talking about statements of a general nature, statements that could be addressed to everybody. But one such statement is: "Thou shalt produce."[6]

In Brecht's lexicon, "production" means something much more than labor (Arbeit) or economic output (Leistung). It evokes both creativity and engagement: it drives an emphatically open-ended, even future-oriented, learning process. In this spirit, then, we could say that acting "according to one's abilities" does not merely deploy some individual set of skills or capacities; instead, it is the most general way of acting, the active element of acting itself, potentially unfolding along multiple lines of becoming, none fixed in advance by physical or mental characteristics. We do not just "have" abilities: we develop them or neglect them in the course of acting them out in relation to others. We do not yet know what we can do, as Deleuze keeps reminding us; the task of *learning what we can do* is barely an obligation: we owe it to ourselves to be able to do something, and so to do more, to do better. In that way, as the *Manifesto* put it, "the free development of each is the condition for the free development of all" and, it must be added, vice versa. This task of "development" or "learning" fulfills without exhausting that most basic wish: to live a better life together with others.

Now look at the second phrase: "to each according to their needs." What, indeed, are our needs? Who or what could ever promise to satisfy them? How strictly do we distinguish between needs and desires? Even the attempt to identify basic needs faces immediate practical complexities: what is most basic? Food, shelter? Two dollars a day? Are our needs grounded in raw necessity, or are they perhaps experienced as an attempt to escape it? The very idea of Utopia will be cast into doubt if we assume that needs are essentially unsatisfiable, whether for social or psychic reasons, or both. Thus Adorno writes in *Minima Moralia*:

> There is tenderness only in the coarsest demand: that no-one shall go hungry any more. Every other seeks to apply to a condition that ought to be determined by human needs, a mode of human conduct adapted to production as an end in itself.[7]

Adorno fears that any elaboration of the notion of needs beyond hunger will justify runaway production, consumerism and all the plagues of the capitalist world. Is hunger, then, a pure need, distinct from all desire? Should we test all of our needs against the standard of hunger, in order to decide which ones are really necessary? This way of talking about needs seems obsolete, and not just because of the expansion in the material resources and productive forces in the decades since Adorno wrote. In fact, the debate over defining and demanding basic needs has shifted from the horizon of perpetual scarcity to the horizon of potential abundance. For the moment, my objection to the perspective of scarcity will take the Utopian path: rather than shrink our needs and demands, we should see how far we might expand them within the sphere of collective satisfaction. The key point is that such "needs" can only be conceived – and satisfied – through the acceptance of a general obligation. Our needs are active and anticipatory, driven by a force of vital persistence and perseverance. Even when they are minimal, our needs animate the full circumference of our lives, touching upon the needs of others at every point.

Now then, how can these two obligations – *to do what we can* and *to provide what we need* – compose a way of life? As I have been suggesting, it is clear that the processes of contribution and provision do not "balance out" at any particular time or place, or for any particular person. (That does not mean that various economic systems have not been planned and presented as if such a reckoning does take place.) Instead, when pursued together, they carry out a mutual expropriation. That is to say, the ethical exercise of abilities *socializes* what would otherwise seem a subjective activity captured by the economic apparatus, while the political satisfaction of needs *individuates* what would otherwise transpire as a more or less fortuitous daily struggle to stay alive. Only by recognizing the incessantly renewed obligations that animate both processes can we hope to retrace and redesign the practices that sustain a common life. Beyond both kinds of obligation, then, there must be something like a form of indebtedness that allows people to share their lives without appropriating each other's possibilities. Seen in light of this task, there is finally no existential or political gap between abilities and needs; that is to say, seen from the perspective of Utopia, both belong to a complex dialectic of agency and apparatus that traverses subjective experience and collective history alike.

A short history of disappointments

Before asking whether these Utopian speculations might prove useful in a moment that seems more dystopian every day, it would be useful to say something about the history of this formulation before and after its citation by Marx.

When Marx's critical notes on the "Gotha Programme," written in 1875, were published by Engels in 1891, well-trained radical readers could hardly have missed the irony that Marx had appropriated this key phrase from the mid-century French politician and "so-called socialist" Louis Blanc. Perhaps half a century had to pass before Blanc's phrase became usable. In fact, Blanc himself had toyed with several versions before coining the decisive one in 1851. Yet Blanc was certainly riffing on slogans coined by the chief disciple of Saint-Simonian socialism, Prosper Enfantin, who framed a social order that aligned "capacities" with "works." The explicitly Christian vocabulary makes clear what might have been legible all along: namely, that this motto of communism is also a mash-up of two passages from the New Testament. As a matter of intellectual history, this lineage might not be surprising at all. What is important for my purposes here is what this echo tells us not only about the religious dimensions of Utopian thinking, but also about the theological structuring of economic thinking itself. As Giorgio Agamben has shown in *The Kingdom and the Glory* and other works, the apparatus of economy combines a rationality of means with a glorification of ends. That is why the articulation or disarticulation of the two phrases remains so difficult: the cultivation of our capabilities must be something other than an instrumentalized means, while the provision of our needs must be something other than an expectation of divine providence.

In spite of – or more likely precisely because of – these deep resonances, Louis Blanc's formula, as relayed by Marx, was installed in a central place in communist politics. Its most famous appearance occurs in Lenin's *State and Revolution*, where it defines the ultimate stage of the revolutionary process itself. Crucially, Lenin holds it up as an as-yet-unrealizable goal, a communism that can be approached only through the less generous, less liberating rigors of socialism. Even this goal is removed by Stalin, who bluntly rewrites the dialectic into a threat, which becomes the supreme law: you must work, and you will be rewarded accordingly. This rewriting, which still seems to pass unnoticed by some of those who cite the phrase, is not at all aberrant. Instead of affirming that to each will be provided according to their need, the prevailing political attitude remains: to each his own. Indeed, "to each his own" is the great anti-Utopian phrase of our times, and it continues to inspire catastrophic deeds.

What is missing in this argument over the rewards of work is any fundamental consideration of the first part of the phrase, namely, the cultivation of capabilities as the condition and goal of radical and Utopian practice. In recent years, this theme has been developed by serious non-Utopian program-makers like Amartya Sen and Richard Sennett. And yet it is precisely the task of a Utopian project to articulate this question of capabilities with the great problem of provision that animated the classic debates about socialism. Today that articulation appears only as a fracture: maybe this is what Jacques Rancière means by "the collectivization of capacities invested in scenes of dissensus."[8]

In a more pragmatic vein, anthropologist and historian of debt David Graeber sees the great slogan as a distillation of an "everyday communism" that animates all societies. (From this perspective, "capitalism is best viewed as a bad way of organizing communism."[9]) Rather than defining some ideal to be realized in the distant future, Graeber suggests, the traffic between abilities and needs simply describes the default mode in which people act and desire, insofar as they are not blocked by hierarchical structures and coercive exchange systems. Debt, as an operation grounded in hierarchy and exchange, has no place in the everyday communism from which genuine democratic projects always draw their strength. In other words, a genuinely free society is one where we can develop our abilities and satisfy our needs without any kind of debt.

In light of this brief history, would-be Utopians have a choice: do you prefer to treat Utopia as a more or less distant project, involving a more or less abrupt interruption of the current order of things and a more or less radical creation of new ways of living? Or do you prefer to think of Utopia as a potentiality that is always and already made actual in our midst, so that, as long as we can recognize it, we may be able to make it happen more often, more deliberately, perhaps even more lastingly?

A short history of aspirations

Let me quickly review the argument so far. We can use Utopian thinking to carry out two distinct but related tasks. First: to imagine alternative social arrangements in the form of Utopian programs: that is the great tradition of Utopian literature from Thomas More until today. Second: to develop the interpretive skills to detect Utopian impulses in all kinds of texts and situations, even dystopian ones, in order to show how wishes disguise themselves in order to keep their chances alive.

We have examined Marx's famous slogan from both angles: as a succinct program-statement for various kinds of socialism and communism, and also as a key to various wishes and impulses that cannot be reckoned by any program. I have tried to show how the call to contribute and the call to provide extend far beyond the usual understanding of "abilities" and "needs," as well as the usual distinction between "obligations" and "desires." In trying to say what we really want for ourselves, and what kind of social ensemble we would actually like to build, it seems that we are inevitably drawn into thinking about bargains: if I do this, what can I expect in return? Must I do anything in particular to deserve a good life? What do I owe the people around me, near and far?

These might appear to be philosophical questions, but they often receive literary answers. Whatever else it may be trying to do, every narrative attempts to inventory and assess a specific set of such bargains. Whole genres – crime stories, love stories – specialize in particular kinds of bargains, while so-called realistic stories carry out a stylization of reality in order to strike a deal with it. It should be possible to develop protocols for reading all kinds of stories as exercises in social bargaining. Here we can turn to a few examples from the Utopian tradition – Utopian program texts – to see how they propose bargains that beggar belief.

The question of work is almost always the first problem to come up, and it is remarkable how often the great Utopian writers insist that work should be both compulsory and voluntary. Thomas More (1516) treats the issue almost in passing, noting that the Utopians have "no cloak or pretence to idleness," given that "they be in the present sight and under the eyes of every man."[10] He details a life full of work: everyone learns to farm, and then takes up some particular craft as a specialty. Labor is thus a matter of virtue, whereby each person reconciles the two imperatives of Utopian life: Epicurean pursuit of pleasure and filial loyalty to the household and the city. Certain officers of the community have no other role than to "take heed that no man sit idle, [so] that every one apply his own craft with earnest diligence."[11]

Yet More recognizes that not everyone is equally virtuous. Those who persist in their idleness, like other kinds of criminals, become "bondmen" who do all kinds of menial labor: they are not free participants in the social bargain, and must submit to continual work and chains. There is still a division of labor in Utopia: not only because of divergent abilities, but because refusal to work is punished by more work. And yet, because everybody works, at least a little, there is greater productivity than under any other system. The generalization of labor is thus rewarded by a generalization of culture, at least for the good citizens of Utopia, who spend their non-working hours attending educational lectures, playing games outdoors, and engaging in "wholesome communication."[12]

We can see clearly how difficult it is for More to convince readers that work might somehow be a pleasure for everybody. To make the trick work, he will have to treat pleasure as a kind of duty, and necessity as a kind of virtue. Likewise, we can see how difficult it is to offer a convincing picture of plentitude to readers who are used to thinking of their needs in terms of scarcity. In order to do that, he makes a pre-emptive strike against luxury and self-indulgence. Here plentitude leads not to hedonism but asceticism, as if it were safe to liberate our needs only when they have been domesticated and rationalized in advance.

In the great nineteenth-century Utopian texts, these motifs will be developed and hardened. Edward Bellamy's *Looking Backward* (1888) takes pains to point out that the centralized socialist economy of the future will allow everyone "to ascertain and follow his natural bent in choosing an occupation" without fear of being materially disadvantaged, because everyone is guaranteed the same amount of purchasing power.[13] Everybody must work, and so everybody wants to work. Those few who do not are imprisoned and fed bread and water until they relent.[14] The more autonomously every individual pursues their abilities, the more fully they will be subsumed by the industrial army itself, which functions as a complete system of contribution and provision: "Every man, however solitary may seem his occupation, is a member of a vast industrial partnership, as large as the nation, as large as humanity. The necessity of mutual dependence should imply the duty and guarantee of mutual support."[15] The phrases fit together tightly. There is no reason to ask which comes first: "mutual dependence" or "mutual support"?; "duty" or "guarantee"? There is no reason to ask because the warehouses are always full, the goods are delivered immediately to your house, and you can never spend all of the credits you have been granted. Bellamy does not say much about what people do with all of their non-working hours: mostly it seems that they listen to the music and sermons piped into the living rooms by the new media technologies.

It is well known that William Morris wrote *News from Nowhere* (1890) to oppose Bellamy's vision. Morris turned the whole problem on its head, portraying a Utopia where needs and desires drive the program, rather than problems of labor and production. It is not efficiency and technological advancement that set the tone, but rather the cultivation of gentleness, civility and beauty. In a future England, after a tumultuous revolution, all the vestiges of the nineteenth-century capitalist system have been wiped out: no more private property, no civil law, no markets in goods or labor, and no state as such. (And, we might add: no more ugly buildings, or clothes or people.) In a society of generalized cooperation, carefully constructed to undo the damage of large-scale industry and to block the re-emergence of competition and strife, each person's working life would be ruled only by the dictates of pleasure. Life itself becomes the highest reward for one's work, thus becoming a work of art in its own right. "There is no difficulty in finding work which suits the special turn of mind of everybody; so that no man is sacrificed to the wants of another."[16] This statement goes even further than Marx: it promises not only that everyone shall be able to pursue their own "special turn of mind," but that the needs of others will not oblige anyone to surrender their own desires. To be obliged to live one's life to the fullest: is that an obligation at all?

By the time we reach the far end of the twentieth century, it is clear just how much sacrifice has been demanded, and how little autonomy offered in return. The most famous American Utopian novels of the 1970s – *The Dispossessed* by Ursula K. Le Guin, and *Trouble on Triton*, by Samuel R. Delany – continue to worry over the reconciliation of work with obligation and need with desire. In Le Guin's novel, two planets provide a direct contrast between an anarchist social order and a hierarchical, competitive one: moments of ascetic selfless solidarity alternate with the nightmarish frenzy of shopping. The Utopian program is thus tested, point by point, against its capitalist enemy, by the novel's protagonist Shevek, a physicist who travels from planet to planet. It is through Shevek's consciousness that some kind of resolution is forged: beyond the bonds of suffering and the allures of refined pleasure, he realizes that the only joy is to be found in maintaining oneself in the flow of time, past and future alike. Thus "loyalty" to one's friends and comrades – the only "we" that matters, on whatever scale – emerges as the Utopian virtue par excellence, an ethical correlate to the physical persistence of the universe that Shevek is hoping to decipher. Delany's book, by contrast, seems constructed to demonstrate how a social order can thrive precisely by encouraging disruption and inconstancy. On Triton, the central problems of work and production recede into the background – some people work, some do not – and instead the focus falls on the elaboration of needs, desires and pleasures. We are given detailed descriptions of the most astonishing aesthetic and sexual performances, and we come to understand that the whole point of having a social order is to make such asocial extravagances possible. It is "anarchist" not because it upholds mutual aid, as in Le Guin, but because it defies authority and normalization of all kinds. Just as Morris replied to Bellamy by emphasizing the Utopian need for beauty in the face of mass economic organization, so Delany replies to Le Guin by stressing the necessarily unreliable passions that compose any social order.

The historian Perry Anderson claims that no Utopian works of "wide resonance" have been produced since the mid-1970s. He links the eclipse of the tradition to the neoliberal "restoration" begun by Thatcher, with her famous anti-Utopian declaration "there is no alternative."[17] Nevertheless, Utopian works continue to be written: witness the recent appearance of Fredric Jameson's *An American Utopia*, a bold and unsettling proposal to imagine how full employment, guaranteed income, universal health care, free education and civil peace might come to the United States. (The quick answer: a "universal army" that includes everyone.) Along the same lines, the science fiction writer Kim Stanley Robinson has proposed a Utopian solution to the economic crisis and the catastrophic effects of climate change, which reads like a checklist of eminently reasonable measures that nevertheless stand no chance of being implemented in the current scheme of things: a Tobin tax on transactions, a Piketty charge on capital assets, a carbon tax and so on. (This Jubilee scenario is played out in his 2017 novel, *New York 2140*.) For Robinson, contrary to Jameson's famous complaint, it is not hard at all to imagine the end of capitalism. In fact, lots of people are talking about the end of capitalism again: not just Wolfgang Streeck, but Paul Mason, Peter Frase, Nick Srnicek and Alex Williams, and, a little earlier, J.K. Gibson-Graham. We would have to sort through these texts to distinguish the various kinds of end in question: disastrous or accelerationist, narrative or paradigmatic, doomed or rescued. Wishing for an end to the present order is getting easier. But wishing for something else is still much harder.

Conclusion

If Utopian thinking remains as complex as that force we call desire – because it is almost indistinguishable from it – it should not be surprising that it takes many forms, wears many masks and gets caught in many ruses. It is worth recalling the three-part triage of desires proposed by Epicurus, a thinker beloved by both More and Marx:

> Of desires, some are *natural and necessary*, some *natural and not necessary*, and some *neither natural nor necessary* but occurring as a result of a groundless opinion.[18]

Knowing how to make these distinctions and act within their principles is already a kind of Utopian program, implying an economy of ascetic restraint, luxurious enjoyment and calm equanimity. Yet it is obvious that his three-part scheme implies a fourth logical position – there are desires that are both *unnatural and necessary*. This seemingly unthinkable possibility opens onto a fully historical arrangement of subjective and collective energies. To be able to articulate what you can do, on the one hand, and what you need, on the other, combining the singular and the plural in an ongoing gesture of thought, is to grasp everyday life under the aspect of Utopia. The "you" who learns what to contribute may not be the same "you" who learns what to provide: the English language allows us to hear the singular and plural oscillating in the pronouns themselves. It is a matter of learning to tune into the elusive wavelengths of our habits, our possessions, our attachments, and our commitments, precisely insofar as such wavelengths are not really ours and do not depend entirely on us. And that is why our Utopian impulses always carry a note of indebtedness, resonating with whatever can and must be done in common. To ears trained only upon the noises of the spectacle, such a sound will seem totally unnatural and unreal, and yet its signal remains insistent, enabling and absolutely necessary.

4. The Politics of Credit

Philip Goodchild
University of Nottingham

Political life is nothing without respect for authority and trust in continuity. In these respects, political power exceeds any foundation in pure force. Violent marauders may come and go, but do not by that means establish sovereign power; on the contrary, they undermine political life. In a famous passage, Thomas Hobbes explained the consequences of living in perpetual fear of random violence:

> In such condition, there is no place for Industry; because the fruit thereof is uncertain; and consequently no Culture of the Earth; no Navigation, nor use of the commodities that may be imported by Sea; no commodious Building; no Instruments of moving, and removing such things as require much force; no Knowledge of the face of the Earth; no account of Time; no Arts, no Letters; no Society; and, which is worst of all, continuall feare, and danger of violent death; And the life of man, solitary, poore, nasty, brutish and short.[1]

This state of fear that endures in what Hobbes calls "a time of war" results in a shortening of time horizons, undermining all commerce, cooperation and culture.[2] Inversely, then, the peace established by sovereign authority is a condition for the creation of wealth through the lengthening of time horizons, establishing trust on the basis of legitimacy. Sovereignty does not consist in the exercise of force alone, for this is merely instantaneous. It involves establishing the continuity of cooperative human endeavor in time through a sense of legitimate authority and a promise of future stability.[3] In these respects, sovereign power is an ongoing performance that demonstrates its legitimacy through its capacity to establish stability. Sovereign power needs to earn its credit.

Sovereign power has, of course, often been established through conquest or through the threat of force. A sovereign is all the stronger who can command many to fight for him, and where such support cannot be compelled, it may be extended by promises of payment, whether from spoils of conquest or from resources gained through taxation and tribute. The more who contribute to establishing power, the stronger the force, and the more stable, in the first instance, is the power established. In short, when sovereign power is guaranteed by a capacity to establish and maintain rule by force, it is usually intimately linked to debt: both the debts of subjects to their sovereign in the form of taxes and tribute, justified by the benefits of establishing legitimate authority, and the debts of the sovereign to soldiers, mercenaries and officers who establish and maintain rule.[4] In this respect, it may be more appropriate to speak of the "debts of politics" as the very conditions for political life, rather than the "politics of debt." There remains, however, a significant problem: sovereign authorities, like violent marauders, live and die. They may fall in battle, be captured by conquerors, usurped by their followers or overcome by sickness. Their debts may remain unpaid, and the peace they establish may be merely temporary. While an individual sovereign offers little continuity, it is far better to fight for a flag that endures. For further continuity may be established by the construction of a state in which successive rulers inherit legitimate authority along with the power to collect taxes and the obligation to honor existing debts. Legitimacy is sustained by honoring promises and debts.[5] In this respect, the upholding of contracts and the handling of debts is among the most fundamental of all political concerns.

One historical illustration of such concerns will have to suffice here. In 1711, the British government reached a crisis in its national debt: it had invested in its navy to prosecute its wars against France and Spain for the sake of increasing its share of the wealth generated through international trade. The debt of £9 million was owed to a multitude of persons: sailors, soldiers, suppliers, craftspeople, victuallers, merchants and money lenders all expected their share, and much of the sum was interest owed on former loans.[6] Parliament had made no provision for this unexpectedly large sum and was somewhat constrained in its choices. The sum was far too large to be raised by taxation; by comparison, the 1696 reminting of the coinage had only sent £5 million in sterling silver back into circulation, and the vast majority of trade was funded on credit.[7] The other option of a default on the debt would lead to economic collapse: with so many creditors being forced in turn to default on their own debts, the debt crisis would spread by contagion. Inaction, by contrast, was leading to a collapse in what was termed the "publick credit," the credit-rating of the state: the government's bills were being sold at discounts of 40 percent, and sailors could only get loans upon them of around 10 percent of their face value, so poorly did merchants anticipate their prospects of payment. Soon the government would no longer be able to borrow at all; it would no longer be able to defend the nation, and with powerful enemies, it risked ceasing to exist. This predicament exemplifies a structural dilemma in the politics of debt: on the one hand, increasing debt extends the power of state sovereignty, giving it enduring existence as the agency responsible for the debt as well as effective power to achieve its designs; on the other hand, increasing debt undermines trust in the public credit once the likelihood of these debts being honored starts to recede. In this case, an audacious and desperate scheme was proposed to solve the dilemma: the South Sea Company was formed to pay off the debts. New investors would receive interest at 6 percent per annum, with any unpaid interest being added to the principal; the money raised in this way would discharge the debt. The profit to pay investors would derive from an unspecified enterprise of trade in the South Seas, no doubt involving some displacement of the Spanish and some colonial settlement, although only 10 percent of the sum invested was allocated to this task, since the remainder was used to pay off the naval debt. The state effectively founded its security on the riskiest form of venture capitalism. As if by a miracle, where holders of government debt had formerly been willing to sell their bonds for 40 percent less than they were owed, enthusiastic new investors in this long-term government debt competed for the opportunity to gain 6 percent in interest.[8] By 1719, with further issues of stock to repay more debt, the popularity of this nationalized project of venture capitalism was such that people invested in the belief that others would continue to invest, the price of the stock would continue to rise, and profits could be made by selling on the inflated stock, rather than such investors having any care for the profitability of the putative South Sea trade. Of course, the speculation that in 1720 erupted in these and other investments eventually caused a price collapse. Nevertheless, the financial revolution still succeeded in consolidating British naval and commercial power.[9] The South Sea Company may have failed, but overall, venture capitalism was capable of producing a sufficient rate of profit to fund the national debt.[10] In this historical instance, as with many others, credible debt was the source of sovereign power. One may therefore understand the "politics of debt" as concerning the decisions that maintain public credit, including the reputation and legitimacy of the sovereign authority.

There is, however, a second dimension to this story. The reason why the price of assets such as the stock of the South Sea Company rose so fast is because investors were able to purchase shares with as little as a 10 percent deposit on the face value of the shares. They bought on margin, with a simple promise of future payment. Share prices went up because the money to pay for them did not yet exist; it was a mere debt, a mere promise. Indeed, so popular were the shares that one could sell them on before the principal payment fell due and pocket the price increase without ever owning assets sufficient to cover the face value. Just as Parliament had promised to settle the naval debt with the promise of future profits, so did investors promise to settle debts with the promise of future profits. In short, the mutual compact of debt between the state and private investors provided legitimacy and stability to the national debt. Sovereign power became all the stronger once it was counterbalanced by the private debts of citizens. The third element in this compact was the banking sector which offered facilities for the settlement of such mutual debts. Banks, like national treasuries and speculative investors, are perpetual debtors, funding the payment and settlement of the debts of others with their own promises or debts. More reliable than a speculator's promise of future payment is an advance offered by a bank. Credit became more reliable and more available when it was regulated by a banking system. A self-stabilizing system of the mutual exchange of debts between private investors, banks and the national state became the basis for political stability and legitimacy. The shared faith in venture capitalism among the state, the people and the financial system became the basis for a stronger state than those founded on taxation and borrowing alone. It also became the basis for investment, and for a stronger economy.

This historical example offers a snapshot of how a system of mutual debts may extend political power beyond the limits of those powers achieved by the threat or use of force and the establishment of legitimacy and stability. It is a system which has considerably strengthened the agency of sovereign power. Contemporary governments also undertake to provide other services such as education, infrastructure, transport facilities, legal regulation, health care, social services, insurance and pensions for their citizens. When the activities of national and local governments typically constitute around 40 percent of GDP in advanced economies, then debt finance is a crucial component alongside taxation in managing the state treasury. Yet such debt-fueled agency is not the prerogative of sovereign power alone. Other forms of agency are also increased by debt: consumers may expand their purchasing power through borrowing; businesses may expand their production and market share through investment; and financial institutions may expand their investments through leverage. Advanced economies operate through high levels of debt throughout all sectors. Each agent trusts in future stability and continuity in order to make promises and undertake debts; each agent contributes to future stability and continuity insofar as their promises are trusted, and their debts are exchanged or used as collateral for further borrowing; and each agent contributes to future stability and continuity by engaging in reliable and predictable behavior that will earn them sufficient income to repay their debt. It is not merely the state that offers a basis for legitimacy and cooperation with others; nor is this derived simply from a market where people trade goods and services. Dependent upon these, yet extending far beyond their powers, is a financial infrastructure of promises, contracts, bonds, obligations and debts. This system of debt provides the peace and stability in which the future may be predicted and long-term plans can be made. Political authority is not confined to the state and those who influence its decisions; it is dispersed among the debtors who build a highly structured existence in which humanity might prosper. For to accept a debt, whether as a new investor or as a means of payment, is to respect the authority of the debtor and to trust in the continuity of their intentions to repay. The repayment of debt is the obligation that founds this dispersed constitution of political power.

This dispersal of sovereign power is hardly democratic: it does not extend to all. In a debt-based economy, agency in the market-place is only available to those who can offer payment with the debts of others, such as the debt of a central or commercial bank, or who can be loaned such debts on the basis of making credible promises themselves, often involving the deposit of collateral. There is a strange dialectic of freedom and constraint at work here. On the one hand, the economic agent is free to exercise choice in the market-place, electing such exchanges and contracts as they deem suitable for their needs and preferences. On the other hand, this sovereign freedom of the economic subject is only achieved by a prior undertaking of such debts and contracts as will provide them with money to spend. Freedom is achieved through self-constraint. Moreover, for those who do not have the collateral, the contacts or the evidence of skills, capabilities and reliable character, the opportunities for earning, employment or borrowing might be severely constrained. Their capacity to subsist may be governed by forced choices. Some may be able to fund their standard of living through borrowing, but can only gain credit from private loan companies that demand high rates of interest, threaten to confiscate property or even have recourse to violence to secure reimbursement. Under such conditions, there is clearly a power relationship in play between creditors and debtors. It is misleading, however, to regard the creditor-debtor relation as a fundamental power relation, for creditors themselves are often debtors in turn in relation to others who fund their lending; alternatively, creditors may be entirely dependent on payment by their debtors who effectively have power over the creditors. The relevant difference in power is a difference in agency in the market-place which determines who can dictate the rate of interest, the deposit of collateral and the terms of trade. It derives from whether choices are purely speculative or are forced. Such agency depends on creditworthiness; it is not the accumulation of wealth alone that determines such agency, but the capacity to draw resources from others by deploying their credit alongside that of one's own. For example, a person who makes a major purchase of a car or a house by offering borrowed money alongside a deposit of their own has a much wider range of choice than those who make purchases simply from their own resources. It is not that creditors control the lives of debtors; in a debt-based economy, those with the most power are those who can borrow more. In this respect, it might be more accurate to speak of a "politics of creditworthiness" rather than a politics of debt.

The conduct which leads to creditworthiness is fairly obvious: punctual settlement of dues, honorable performance of contracts, care to show goodwill at the slightest hint of customer dissatisfaction, and fair and upright dealing. A society where agency is founded on debt contracts is a society which propagates a particular kind of morality.[11] Moreover, insofar as others are connected in a web of credit relations and depend upon one's ability to enter into exchanges and contracts, one's ability to make settlement on time and one's ability to insure or borrow against random misfortune, then personal morality is a matter of public interest. Enthusiasm, aspiration, commitment, concentration, punctuality, obedience, flexibility and integrity are the moral qualities upon which credit and public welfare are founded; they are evoked, in turn, by the harsh consequences and forced choices available to those who fail to inspire credit. In this respect, the power relations of creditworthiness serve to propagate a morality which is to the advantage of creditors and employers. If, for some, the converse appears to hold, that those who fail to attract credit may be suspected of moral failings such as indolence, lack of ambition, inability to honor one's word, being subject to distraction, tardiness, disobedience, obstinacy and dishonesty, then the forced choices may seem the most appropriate moral reward as well as the most appropriate moral discipline for re-establishing integrity. Nevertheless, the actual integrity of the relatively powerless is not at stake here, nor is the difficulty of maintaining a culturally dominant morality under the unstable conditions of life of those who are subject to forced choices. That some lives are lived within debt-based venture capitalism under conditions that resemble Hobbes' description of the instability of the state of war, where it is hard to invest in the future for fear of random violence or misfortune, does not earn such people any credit. For creditworthiness does not consist in integrity itself, but in a reputation for integrity;[12] it is not the property of the individual. Likewise, those who lack credit may not need to labor to establish moral integrity itself but merely a reputation for integrity. Venture capitalism, with its promise of future profits, turns inwards: it becomes a faith in the future wealth to be obtained from those inner South Seas which are moral qualities such as enthusiasm, aspiration, commitment, concentration, punctuality, obedience, flexibility and integrity. For debtors and creditors alike, the reputation for such qualities is a necessary yet insufficient condition for access to wealth. Just as a sovereign power only increases its agency by constraining itself by debt, so also do sovereign individuals construct their freedom from self-constraint. The complex constraints placed upon the states responsible for their national debts are redoubled for their citizens.

Overall, then, the wealth of a nation, founded on a compact of mutual debts between states, private investors and financial infrastructure, remains at once stabilizing yet fragile. Of course, it remains the case that the strength of a nation depends upon its power to collect taxes, and this in turn depends upon a willingness to be taxed on the part of its populace and a healthy economy that can yield profits. National policy is only viable if it conforms to such conditions. It also remains the case that the strength of a nation depends upon its capacity to borrow, its credit-rating, and this is turn depends upon a healthy economy where the most secure investment is deemed to be the national debt itself, which consequently pays the lowest interest rate. National policy is only viable if it conforms to the beliefs of the bond market about what will produce the most secure economy.

Yet the wealth of a nation also depends upon the capacity of its citizens to borrow, for without such borrowing, there would be no investment, no commerce, no profits, no capital, no money, no taxes and no lending. National policy is only viable if it attends to the credit of the public, promoting a culture for the reputation of moral probity. So citizens contribute to the stability of political life not only as taxpayers, as workers yielding profits, or as investors, but also as borrowers. In this last respect, the strength and stability of a nation depends upon the moral life of its citizens. Yet in each of these respects, sovereign political freedom becomes subordinated to the interests of corporate and financial power.

It cannot, however, be said that the ghosts of violent marauders have been exorcized by such complex means. Nations and economies founded on debt may live with the perpetual threat of crisis. There are external threats, such as war or environmental crisis. There are internal economic threats, such as hyper-inflation, speculative bubbles, credit crises or debt-deflation. There are internal political threats, such as the populace refusing to accept the policy that seems most appropriate to the financial markets. There is also a moral threat: a loss of faith in borrowing as the route to stability may result in either a direct reduction in borrowing or a reduction in the behavior that is deemed creditworthy. The ghosts of violent marauders have invaded within. In one respect, for those who are being forcibly disciplined into becoming moral subjects and worthy borrowers, the state itself may appear to have become a gang of violent marauders. The artificial instability of their lives may prevent the future planning that it was designed to produce. While the creditworthy attributes may be comparatively easy for those with access to careers and prospects to maintain, insecurity undermines faith.

In the long run, however, a state needs taxes, investors and private debtors for its own stability. It may not need all its citizens.

If the mass of citizens proves incapable in these respects, then the burden of these roles may be shouldered by those successful and reliable corporations that occupy the principal positions in the productive and financial economies. For corporations can manifest creditworthy moral qualities far more effectively than individuals; like sovereign states, they endure beyond the employment of any of their directors. Where the many can contribute less due to their conditions of disorganization, the few can contribute more. When the next credit crisis strikes, and further unpayable debts need to be consolidated as permanent once more by a collective agreement between state treasuries, central banks and private enterprise, there will be few compelling reasons to attend to the interests of citizens. If their lives have to become just a little more nasty, brutish and short, this might simply be the requirements of the next phase of debt-based state capitalism. After all, this is a price that is already being borne by other species on this planet. If the only alternative on offer is the collapse of both the economy and the state, resulting in Hobbes' war of all against all, then, to some, such sacrifices might seem to be a price worth paying. For now that there are few external South Seas as sources of imagined wealth, this tendency toward a shrinking of horizons has become the new trajectory of the politics of debt. Yet the fundamental contradiction of such a politics of debt is that it is built upon the foundation of a faith in a future that it can no longer produce. Once such faith fails, then the world will need to build legitimacy and stability upon a very different faith.

The crucial issue, here, is whether increasing borrowing, be it by the state, private sector or financial infrastructure, is always sufficient to generate future wealth. An essential economic resource, enabling investment, borrowing and even modern money itself, is faith in future prosperity achieved through economic cooperation. Cooperation is founded upon faith in a future, yet this future is to be achieved through cooperation itself.

Capitalism must collapse without such faith. In this respect, global market capitalism as a whole bears some structural resemblance to an investment bubble like that of the South Sea Company: it feeds its own growth through expectation where all debts are the leverage that fuels growth. For some time, it does not matter whether the asset is in reality over-valued, for so long as others are investing in expectation that the price will rise, then, in the short-term, the price will rise and profits can be made. For the condition for the emergence of an investment bubble is the use of leverage or trading on margin so that an investor provides only a proportion of the nominal asset price. In other words, a debt, a simple promise of future payment, may be a source of demand growth.

In general, speculative bubbles do not continue to expand indefinitely. One may still distinguish between the underlying fundamentals which offer grounds for faith and the increase in borrowing that expresses such faith. The ground for faith in future prosperity is the power of increasing exchange, including the mobility of goods, services, labor and capital, as the route toward economic growth. For individuals, this faith in exchange is supported by three key elements: hope for future prosperity, based on evidence of increasing wealth; faith in the stability of the global financial system, as the infrastructure mediating investment, borrowing and exchange; and effective wealth distribution, for exchange can only be trusted as a route to accumulation if there is a realistic chance of obtaining wealth. If economic growth starts to falter, then income and profits can only be drawn by some at the expense of others. Once the future no longer appears to be a reservoir of prosperity, a source of motivation for investing credit and a source of collateral for undertaking debt, then a far more defensive political dynamic will start to emerge.

The key problem here is that debt is ambivalent: in the first instance it increases demand and investment, but subsequently debt service acts as a drag upon demand and investment. Debt may continue to grow whether an economy itself grows or shrinks. One mechanism works like this: when debt is issued against collateral, such as a mortgage based on the value of a house, then the quantity of debt is fixed, while the property will fluctuate with market value.[13] In a downturn, when asset prices fall because there is a rush to sell, debt remains fixed. After a downturn, wealth decreases but debts do not; the level of debt remains stuck at a new, higher rate, while there is less wealth in the economy to support it. Likewise, when people deleverage and pay down their debts, they reduce the amount of money circulating in the economy. Demand goes down and businesses contract, leading to unemployment, less investment and less income from which debts can be serviced. In Irving Fisher's description of a debt-deflationary spiral, the more debtors pay off, the more they owe.[14] In other words, whether the economy grows or shrinks, the level of private debt to GDP stays ratcheted up.

These dynamics have been given a mathematical description by the Australian economist Steve Keen, who has shown that the aggregate demand that drives an economy is given by the sum of GDP plus the growth in credit.[15] In other words, while a growing economy can drive itself, with money circulating faster and faster, an economy can also be driven by an increase in private debt, for this is new money creation that adds to demand even when this exceeds the rate of growth. Credit creation is the volatile factor here. If private debt is small relative to GDP then changes in borrowing habits have less significance within a growing economy; yet once private debt is large relative to GDP, a change in borrowing can easily outweigh any previous GDP growth. Keen suggests that the key threshold is when private debt reaches about 150 percent of GDP.[16] Beyond this threshold any economic downturn paralyzes an economy such that aggregate debt repayment becomes impossible, and the demand for increasing credit falls away. If the first such "zombie economy" was Japan, it has been joined by several others since 2008, and even China looks likely to follow.

The underlying point is that global market capitalism is fueled by debt and there are internal, mathematical limits to debt-driven economic growth. Once overall levels of debt rise, most funds are directed toward debt service, crowding out both consumption and investment. As debts are repaid, overall demand shrinks, followed by reductions in overall rates of production and profit, making it harder to reduce debts any further. The economy stagnates and profits can only be earned by the extraction of wealth from others. Such extraction is not new, but it had previously been disguised by the promise of inclusion in wealth creation through the globalization of knowledge, skills, productive capacity and governance.

The clearer the evidence becomes for stagnating prosperity, financial instability and rising inequality, then the less authority will be granted to an ideal of globalized exchange with its promises of future wealth. Cooperation is less forthcoming when future prosperity is no longer on offer. In short, we stand at the threshold of a crisis of faith for the politics of credit and debt. It is not simply a matter of the credit-ratings of sovereign states and their subservience to institutional investors, nor is it simply a matter of the disciplined life produced by all individuals who are in debt. Sovereign debts are secured not only by their lenders and taxpayers but also by those private borrowers and speculators whose debts circulate in the same economy as treasury bonds. Once the circle of reliable debtors shrinks to a few state, corporate and financial institutions, then it no longer offers a source of prosperity and longer time horizons for the populace at large. Once political authorities lose their capacity to promise future stability, then they lose their aura of legitimacy. A sovereign state that lacks any putative South Seas will be considerably diminished in its power. Founding political life on the riskiest forms of venture capitalism, although immensely successful for 3 centuries, may prove to be just a bubble.

One may easily imagine some of the tendencies that might emerge from a future credit crisis:

1. The tightening of an economy of extraction, where a few institutions extract more and more for less in return, making life more precarious for all kinds of workers.
2. A defensive political reaction in the form of attempts to retain the share of a shrinking pot by particular interest groups, departing from the wider cooperation and prosperity achieved through globalization.
3. A powerless but increasingly vocal movement to return to local, subsistence, and steady-state economies which finds itself in conflict with the aims and interventions of the previous two strategies.
4. In place of faith in a prosperous, secular future, one may even see a repetition of the kind of triumph enjoyed by world religions in the majority world throughout the twentieth century where life has been insecure and unstable. If there is no other future hope, one may even see the return of religion in the heartlands of secularization.

What is less clear is how any clashes between or within such tendencies will play out in practice. Yet political life is nothing without respect for authority and trust in continuity. Neither pure force, pure wealth nor pure debt will be capable of deciding the issue. For power depends upon cooperation, and cooperation depends upon faith. If debt proves to be an inadequate ground for faith, then humanity will have to look elsewhere for a faith that regulates its conduct and grants it stability.

5. The "Bitter Necessity" of Debt: Neoliberal Finance and the Society of Control

Steven Shaviro

In an essay originally published some 20 years ago, Gilles Deleuze argues that we are in the process of moving away from Michel Foucault's disciplinary society, and toward a new sort of social formation, which Deleuze calls the control society. The disciplinary society operates "by organizing major sites of confinement," such as family, school, barracks, factory and prison. In this system, "individuals are always going from one closed site to another, each with its own laws."[1] But at the end of the twentieth century, Deleuze writes, "we're in the midst of a general breakdown of all sites of confinement." Instead, "ultrarapid forms of apparently free-floating control...are taking over from the old disciplines at work within the time scales of closed systems."[2]

The differences between these two forms of social organization are numerous. Where the disciplinary society was analogical, the control society is digital.[3] Where the disciplinary society applied rigid molds as forms of confinement, the control society works like "a modulation, like a self-transmuting molding continually changing from one moment to the next, or like a sieve whose mesh varies from one point to another."[4] Where the disciplinary society "molds the individuality" of each person, the control society addresses us instead as what Deleuze calls dividuals.[5] That is to say, our identities are multiple, and they are continually being decomposed and recomposed, on various levels, through the modulation of numerous parameters.[6] There's my credit-rating, and my medical record, and the databases that track my Visa card use and my web browsing habits. Each of these identifies me separately, for particular purposes. Where the disciplinary society relies upon my signature as a guarantee of my fixed identity, the control society relies instead upon passwords that regulate my differential access to one service or another. Deleuze suggests that, underlying all these other contrasts, "money, perhaps, best expresses the difference between the two kinds of society, since discipline was always related to molded currencies containing gold as a numerical standard, whereas control is based on floating exchange rates, modulations depending on a code setting sample percentages for various currencies."[7]

The transition from discipline to control is an ongoing process of long duration. Indeed, it is never the case that one system entirely effaces the other, but rather that elements of the older system persist within the overall framework of the newer one. Nonetheless, we can perhaps symbolically date the transition from discipline to control to August 15, 1971. This is the date on which Richard Nixon ended the convertibility of US dollars to gold, thereby ushering in the system of floating exchange rates that we have today. To summarize the differences between these two social formations, we may say that, where the disciplinary society is closed and hierarchical, the control society is open, fluid and rhizomatic. Moreover, this difference in form is also a difference between the characteristic media of each. I am using "media" here in Marshall McLuhan's sense; they are not just means of production and expression, but material and processual arrangements that are "extensions of some human faculty – psychic or physical," and that "work us over completely...leave no part of us untouched, unaffected, unaltered."[8] Media are extrapolated from our bodies; and they redound back upon our bodies and our sensoria. The ways that disciplinary institutions affected the human body are now well known – consider, for instance, how Taylorism and the assembly line molded the habits of generations of workers. In contrast, we do not yet entirely know just how the control society is changing our postures, our gestures and our perceptions: though the proliferation of screens and data access points throughout private and public space, the growing importance of gestural and tactile interfaces, and the spread of multitasking all provide clues.

In Deleuze's terms, the two types of society are organized around two different sorts of technologies, or machines. "Disciplinary societies were equipped with thermodynamic machines," he says, whereas "control societies function...with information technology and computers."[9] This means that disciplinary societies operate directly on human bodies and physical objects, by managing the flows of energy that pass through them. Control societies, in contrast, work by abstracting bodies and objects into data; they can then command the movements of these bodies and objects by manipulating their data. Thermodynamic machines are continually battling against entropy, and they can be directly subverted by sabotage; whereas informational machines are continually battling against noise, and they can be subverted by "piracy and viral contamination." All in all, the social shift from discipline to control involves a technological shift from energetics to informatics, as the crucial means for organizing social interactions, and for generating, expropriating and accumulating wealth. Of course, "thermodynamic machines" like heavy industrial plants – not to mention automobiles – haven't disappeared from our information-centric world, and are not likely to in the foreseeable future. People still drive cars; and now they need to buy computing and communications hardware as well. If places like the American Midwest have been deindustrialized, this is because factories and sweatshops have merely been transferred to "developing" countries like China, Mexico and Indonesia, where the wage rate is much lower.

Nevertheless, the transition from the disciplinary to the control society marks a radical change in the way that physical production is organized and governed. Deleuze carefully points out that "this technological development is more deeply rooted in a mutation of capitalism."[10] He goes on to show how the transition from discipline to control is coordinated with the major changes in capitalism that other commentators have noted: the transition from the welfare state to the neoliberal state; from Taylorism to Toyotaism; from Fordism to post-Fordism and flexible accumulation[11]; from demands for obedience on the part of workers to demands that workers be adaptable, flexible, versatile and "entrepreneurial"[12]; from industrial capital and "material expansion" to finance capital and "financial expansion"[13]; and from the formal to the real subsumption of labor under capital.[14] Michel Foucault himself, despite his thinly veiled hostility to Marxism, nonetheless comes to many of the same conclusions as Deleuze. The one place where Foucault overtly considers the question of what comes after the disciplinary society is in *The Birth of Biopolitics*[15], his 1978-1979 lecture series at the Collège de France. Despite his title and his initial premises, Foucault ends up not speaking about biopolitics at all. He doesn't even say much about the ostensibly central subject of his late philosophical reflections: what he calls "governmentality"[16] or "the art of government."[17] Instead of tracing the disciplinary logic of the management of bodies and populations, Foucault in these lectures looks at what was then only starting to be called "neoliberalism." Specifically, he describes the construction of a new figure of Homo oeconomicus, far different from the familiar figure of the eighteenth century. With the icy objectivity of an entomologist describing the habits of parasitic wasps, Foucault outlines the emerging logic of "human capital," and its "investment" in conditions of supposed scarcity.

Classical liberalism was founded upon a logic of exchange: what Adam Smith conceived as the universal human "propensity to truck, barter and exchange one thing for another." In Foucault's terms, "the characteristic feature of the classical conception of

Homo oeconomicus is the partner of exchange and the theory of utility based on a problematic of needs."[18] But according to Foucault, neoliberalism is founded upon a radically new logic: "a shift from exchange to competition in the principle of the market... the most important thing about the market is competition, that is to say, not equivalence but on the contrary inequality." For the neoliberals, "competition, and only competition, can ensure economic rationality."[19] In consequence of this, the neoliberals propose a new image of Homo oeconomicus. Now "he is not at all a partner of exchange," but rather "an entrepreneur, an entrepreneur of himself...being for himself his own capital, being for himself his own producer, being for himself the source of [his] earnings."[20] In thus presenting a new vision of economic man, Foucault says, neoliberalism effects "an inversion of the relationships of the social to the economic."[21] Instead of seeing political economy as just one facet of a broader social landscape, neoliberal logic regards all social phenomena as resulting from the economic calculations and investment decisions of individual actors. As Foucault puts it, neoliberalism "involves, in fact, the generalization of the economic form of the market. It involves generalizing it throughout the social body and including the whole of the social system not usually conducted through or sanctioned by monetary exchanges."[22] This means that all social phenomena and relations, without exception, "are analyzed in terms of investment, capital costs, and profit... on the capital invested."[23] Even such things as "marriage, the education of children, and criminality"[24] must be conceived in this way. Economic analysis can be applied to any and all human conduct that "reacts to reality in a non-random way."[25] This is to say that market logic can be applied – and should be applied, according to neoliberal dogma – to all human activity and behavior whatsoever.

Following Foucault, we can thus trace three stages in the development of bourgeois institutions and bourgeois political thought. In the mid-seventeenth century, Thomas Hobbes posited the authoritarian state as the one and only entity capable of founding civil society, by ending the otherwise incessant war of all against all. This provides a rationale for what Foucault calls the society of sovereignty. In the latter part of the eighteenth century, Adam Smith argued that manufacture, commerce and trade, fueled by the propensity to exchange, offered a smoother way to suspend the war of all against all, and thereby to allow civil society to flourish. This is the position of classical liberalism. The role of the state is to promote the peaceful conditions for industry and trade, and for the increasing specialization of labor. And the division of labor, in turn, provides the material basis for what Foucault calls the disciplinary society. But twentieth- and twenty-first-century neoliberalism inverts this whole tradition. For neoliberalism, the legitimate role of the state is precisely to destroy civil society, and instead to incite a war of all against all, in the form of unfettered economic competition. Where Hobbes sees the war of all against all as a primordial condition that we need to escape from, neoliberalism sees the war of all against all as a desirable state that does not arise spontaneously, but needs to be actively engendered. And where Smith finds a harmony between the pursuit of self-interest and the natural human tendency toward sympathy, neoliberalism seeks to extirpate the latter, in order to compel human beings to act in accordance with the former. This is why, as Margaret Thatcher so notoriously put it, "there is no such thing as society" in the neoliberal vision; "there are individual men and women, and there are families." It would be absurd to criticize neoliberalism for failing to recognize the social; for in fact, the extermination of the social – or of any form of relation of broader scope than that of the family – is precisely the goal of neoliberal policy.

It is in this context that neoliberalism claims to dispose of the whole problem of labor and exploitation. The antagonism between capital and labor has, of course, haunted capitalism since the very beginning. All the conditions that Marx explicitly noted in his analysis of capitalism were already implicitly acknowledged in the work of Smith and Ricardo. And as a practical matter, problems arising from the conflict of interests between labor and capital continued to trouble capitalism for most of the twentieth century. But neoliberalism eliminates this tension by simply redefining it out of existence. When I sell my labor-power as a commodity, receiving in return money as the means for a certain level of subsistence, what I am really doing, according to the neoliberals, is "investing" my "human capital" in the competitive market-place, and receiving a return on this investment.

We are now, Foucault says, "at the opposite extreme of a conception of labor power sold at the market price to a capital invested in an enterprise. This is not a conception of labor-power; it is a conception of capital-ability," formulated in such a way that "the worker himself appears as a sort of enterprise for himself."[26] Economic competition as an endless war of all against all thus entirely displaces class antagonism. Of course, I don't mean to imply that a theoretical redefinition, in and of itself, has the power to change the way that things are organized and managed in the world. Workers are still being exploited – which is to say, a surplus is still being extracted from their labor – regardless of how this process is described. But this does not mean that neoliberal dogma is simply mystification, or ideology. Rather, we should see the theoretical shifts dissected by Foucault as performative utterances. The expression of such theories is a particular sort of action, which is coordinated with other kinds of political, social and economic actions. The rise of neoliberalism as a mode of understanding goes together with the actual destruction of labor unions, and the deregulation of financial markets, that took place under the rule of Reagan and Clinton, and Thatcher and Blair. In other words, although neoliberal dogma is not "true," it is nonetheless frighteningly effective. It does not provide an alibi for exploiting workers, so much as it positively works to make the status of the worker, and the process of labor-as-exploitation, literally unthinkable. It makes the very things that I am saying now seem hokey, old-fashioned and flat-out unbelievable – even to myself.

Neoliberalism has entered into all our preconscious assumptions; it permeates our habits of thought and speech. Even when we seek to oppose the most outrageous depredations of human livelihoods and of the physical environment, we find ourselves using the language and the presuppositions of cost-benefit analysis, optimization and so on. We no longer have the language to articulate radical demands. We suffer from a failure of imagination. As Fredric Jameson and Slavoj Žižek have both suggested, we find it easier today to imagine the total extermination of human existence than to imagine a humane alternative to global capitalism. In the course of *The Birth of Biopolitics*, Foucault explicitly states that the neoliberal regime cannot be explained in terms of the disciplinary society and its "normative mechanisms."[27] Rather, he says, neoliberalism involves "the image, idea, or theme-program of a society in which there is an optimization of systems of difference, in which the field is left open to fluctuating processes," and "in which there is an environmental type of intervention instead of the internal subjugation of individuals."[28] To the best of my knowledge, this is the one and only place where Foucault explicitly theorizes a post-disciplinary social arrangement. And his formulations are quite close to Deleuze's later formulations regarding the control society. Both accounts see the multiplication of differences, and the continuing "optimization," or "modulation" of loose, "fluctuating processes" as a practice of control.

To summarize, both Foucault, in his analysis of neoliberalism, and Deleuze, in his analysis of the control society, insist upon what I can only call an economism at the heart of postmodernity. I use this word advisedly. "Economism" has long been a cardinal sin in Marxist and progressive circles. And, looking more widely, many people on the Left have rejected or criticized Marxism precisely because of its insistence upon the economic in the "last instance" – even if, as per Althusser, "the lonely hour of the 'last instance' never comes."[29] Deleuze, and especially Foucault, are often associated with these criticisms; their work opened up other ways, more indebted to Nietzsche than to Marx, of considering power, desire and the social. And yet, when Deleuze and Foucault contemplate the futurity knocking at the door, they both rediscover the force of the economic, returning with a vengeance. Far from focusing on biopower or biopolitics, Foucault abandons this direction of his thought. He suggests – contrary to so much of the theorizing that has been done in his name in the years since his death – that we cannot understand contemporary society in terms of the supposed postulation of "life" as a target and focus of power. We need to follow the proliferation of market logic instead.

As for Deleuze, far from being the rapturous poet of flows, rhizomatic structures and open systems that he is so often taken to be, he explicitly warns us that these new, flexible forms of social organization in fact have their own traps, their own mechanisms of oppression, their own devices of exploitation and subordination. Almost in spite of themselves, both Deleuze and Foucault rediscover political economy at the heart of social processes that had previously seemed to be of an entirely different order. And this is where we get – finally – to the question of debt. Under the logic of neoliberalism and the control society, the traditional disciplinary regimes of schools, factories and so on lose their power; they are replaced by the so-called "discipline of the market," with its accounting for all areas of human life in financial terms. Everything is now subject to market competition – or to what the godfather of neoliberalism, Friedrich von Hayek, called "the bitter necessity of [man's] submitting himself to rules he does not like in order to maintain himself against competing groups."

The financialization of human life means that market competition, with its calculus of credit and debt, is forcibly built into all situations, and made into a necessary precondition for all potential actions. Nietzsche traced the transformation of a primordial indebtedness into such things as interiority and guilt. But today, this process seems to have been reversed; interiority and guilt, like everything else, are analyzed back into indebtedness. Debt has become our universal condition, and the "servicing" of debt – that is to say, the extraction of payments for debt – has become a major resource for capital accumulation in the world today. As Deleuze says, in the control society "a man is no longer a man confined but a man in debt."[30] For neoliberalism and the control society – if not necessarily for Adam Smith and the disciplinary society – the "free market" functions as an instrument of control. The objective function of the market is that it "forces us to be free," forces us to behave "rationally" and "efficiently," forces us to act concertedly in our own individual interests – any broader considerations be damned. Ethics, aesthetics, sympathy, solidarity and care for others are all simply excluded, except to the extent that they can be packaged as commodities and put up for sale. The "price system" continually forces us into debt. And thereby it confines, restricts and channels our behavior far more rigidly, and effectively, than any compulsion based upon mere brute force would be able to do.

One of the lessons of the twentieth century has been that totalitarian regimes tend to have short lives. No matter how rigid and repressive they endeavor to be, they tend toward a point of implosion, at which they consume themselves. So far in our experience, an expansive and predatory capitalism is the only system that has found a way to perpetuate itself by means of its own inequities and crises. No state apparatus, no "governmentality," no measure of surveillance, and no form of education or propaganda has been able to constrain human freedom as comprehensively – or as invisibly – as the neoliberal market has done. If the economic collapse of 2008 has demonstrated that the capitalist debt economy is not viable in the long term, it has nonetheless also become an alibi, and a mechanism, for extending the reach of this economy even further. Ultimately, financial debt is a way of colonizing and pre-empting (or premediating, in Richard Grusin's term) the future, of pricing its unknowability according to a measure that is graspable and controllable in the present – despite the fact that such a practice is madness and delusion, since the future is intrinsically unknowable and unpredictable. In this sense, capitalist debt as we know it today is a kind of double process. It ravages the present in the name of a future that will never actually arrive; and it depletes our hopes for, and imaginings of, the future by turning it into nothing but a projection and endless repetition of the present.

6. Debt: Managing an Impossible Inheritance

Elettra Stimilli
Sapienza University of Rome

One might think debt relates exclusively to an economic transaction similar to an exchange, where what has been borrowed is returned in accordance with the conditions agreed. In fact, debt creates a more complex relationship. It involves an obligation. At the origin of this obligation, a relationship similar to the one that, in religion, unites men to gods has been identified: a relationship of dependency toward superior powers, in which the living are obliged to redeem, during their lifetimes, the vital energy of which they were made custodians.[1] The most ancient form of redemption used for repaying the debt of life to the gods is sacrifice.[2] The power associated with the cult of sacrifice concentrates on the victim, in whom the seeds of dissent that are present within a given society are polarized to alter its course.[3]

As an obligation, debt is fundamentally an expression of a social bond. To break it would imply guilt, the wrong of failing to comply with established conditions or to meet one's obligations. At the same time, this bond reveals a capacity to act as an effective instrument of power. Indeed, it is clear that the expression "to be in debt" does not mean merely "to have some debts." It expresses something that one cannot, in fact, own, but instead something by which one is owned and to which one is subjugated. Literally, "to be in debt" means "to owe a debt of life" that cannot be overcome because it dominates.

Today more than ever, "being in debt" coincides with a situation into which it is impossible to enter only at a given moment, because it is determined by an inheritance one acquires before even coming into existence, by the condition into which one is born, regardless of how poor or privileged one's circumstances may be. Even those who have never voluntarily acquired debts are born indebted, in states that transmit debt to citizens even before they are born. Of course, depending on the geographic, political and social context and according to how much state protection is present, the role and importance of debt also change. For example, a young African migrant who manages to reach the shores of Italy alive (an increasingly difficult feat following the agreements signed between Italy and Libya in the summer of 2017 with the support of Europe's main powers) is forced for several years to repay the debt he incurred to those who transported him. American students, long before they start working, find themselves indebted to banks that provide money for the payment of their university fees, and they already know that for many years they will have to allocate a part of their earnings to repaying this debt.

In any event, today as never before, we see that debt cannot only precede life in terms of time but can also determine it, even exposing it to the risk of death, as demonstrated by the high rate of suicides motivated by debt recorded during the financial crisis.[4] In this context, one could say that debt is an inheritance that, in a way, cannot be rejected or that, in any event, is extremely difficult to manage.

In recent years, debt has been explicitly tied to guilt, to failing to meet commitments undertaken, especially in light of the European Union finding itself directly involved in the global financial crisis. The question of debt has therefore become a specific problem for some European nations, which are considered responsible for poor management of the state. In this sense, it has been a guilt that is easily attributable to and equally easy to position in the context of what can be amended, in the category of damage that has been caused, a broken rule or a breached agreement, which, however, can be compensated through making sacrifices.

Recent policies for economic regeneration and recovery, critical of the system behind the austerity regime, have explicitly opposed the blame-engendering paradigm of austerity and offered themselves as alternatives. But more than a real alternative, these approaches, which promote economic development, are a symptom of the opacity that still needs to be explored and is at the origin of a much larger problem requiring fresh analyses.

Today, debt does not appear so much as, and only as, a condition to be altered – as the authoritarian order for the sacrifices imposed by austerity policies would seem to imply – nor simply as the last and empty expression of a legal bond. We need, therefore, to understand the nature of its role in current global policy, considering the centrality it continues to have across the world, despite the changes to global equilibrium that have occurred since the beginning of the financial crisis in 2008.

The global market and new legal institutions

Since Europe found itself directly involved in the global financial crisis, we have seen debt discussed in the media as if it were a form of guilt.[5] The "German model" has turned out to promote a blame-engendering vision of the public debt incurred by some European Union countries. According to this interpretation, the situation in which some southern European states have found themselves is the result of national economic mismanagement, which is easily attributable and punishable.

It is worth asking, however, what is really at stake here. That is, we must understand whether considering debt as a guilt *effectively* means locating the state of widespread indebtedness within the context of what can be changed, in the category of a damage caused, a broken rule or a breached agreement, which, however, can be compensated through "sacrifices," as those in charge of European austerity policies have wanted us to believe.

More than a technical economic issue, the problem of debt

has shown itself to be a powerful political instrument. What is at stake, however, does not seem to be so much, or only, a dimension of power in which the establishment of law is based solely on discipline, on repression and the resulting sense of guilt. More is at work, therefore, than juridical measures that engender blame. Rather, new regulatory institutions operate with different methods of repression and through new conditions that create debt.

With the affirmation of neoliberal policies, the market became the dominant political institution. This phenomenon produced a radical transformation in terms of normative production. The function of guilt linked to the economy of debt changed with the shifting conditions that produced it. The categories at the heart of this transformation are no longer only those of a juridical nature, which nowadays control national states. From the moment the market became the dominant political institution, the economic categories connected to the field of valuation were at stake. In this context, guilt is not only the expression of an unmet obligation. Instead, it involves the condition that is produced at the moment when, with neoliberal policies, the ways of giving value to life fully match the valorization of capital, thus making it possible for each person to become "human capital," and therefore to be (or not be) worthy of the investment expected, and thus finding himself, in this second case, in the condition of one who feels guilty.

The concept of "human capital" has featured in economic theory since the 1960s and has also begun to receive significant attention in the social context.[6] "Human capital" includes skills, knowledge, abilities and ways of interacting, things normally connected more to the ethical context than to economics. These attributes have been placed within the logic of the market, thus transforming it. Other factors contributing to the growth and formation of human capital are the family and social contexts, education, work experience and forms of consumption. Even though they cannot be measured separately, the components of human capital have a decisive influence on the quality of the service provided by the person who holds them, facilitating an increase in productivity and an enhancement of the company, which influence the latter's results. Investment in human capital means sustaining the costs of developing the knowledge and abilities of individuals (for example, paying teaching expenses).

We can create an analogy between human capital and non-human capital (such as equipment, installations, etc.). In the same way that investments in non-human capital are intended to increase production capacity and business revenue, investments in human capital aim to increase the production capacity and revenue of individuals, who are considered, in this context, as genuine enterprises. The fundamental difference between the two concerns property rights. While property rights to non-human capital can clearly be exchanged on the market, human capital, on the one hand, belongs exclusively to the individual who holds it, while on the other, it is never identified as property in the strict sense – because it is not entirely quantifiable, it is difficult to transfer through a normal sale-purchase agreement.

Consequently, a profound transformation took place in the capitalist modes of production at the moment in which this type of entrepreneurial rationality tied to the concept of human capital was extended to all work environments and across the social and political arenas until it affected the entire existences of millions of people, who as individuals became "items of capital" in which investments could be made. The enterprise-form established itself and the "entrepreneur of himself"[7] became the prototype to which all the key figures in a typical economy – the "worker", the "manufacturer" and the "consumer" – adapted themselves.[8] This move led to a radical questioning of the classical distinction between "action" and "production." The worker, manufacturer and consumer were not only united by the fact of all having become "entrepreneurs," they were also all engaged in enhancing their "human capital" to the greatest extent, thus further implicating the ethical dimension linked to praxis in the context of production.

If the productive subject, the *homo faber*, is the most striking result of modern industrial society, which had as a counterpart in the process a force that was equally productive, efficient and concerned with constructing useful individuals who were docile workers, inclined to consume, but also devoted to sacrifice, then the dominance of neoliberalism is characterized by the hegemony of the model of the commercial enterprise. According to business logic, human lives are integrally involved in the activities to which they are assigned. This implies the total participation of individual desires in those activities. Their gratification is not confused with the satisfaction of essential needs linked to survival, nor is it deferred through sacrifices. Instead, it concerns individual lives in a broader sense, connected to an ethical space of existence, where everyone becomes, precisely, "entrepreneur of himself."

The "entrepreneur of himself" is an active subject who dedicates himself entirely to the activity to which he is assigned, trying to suppress any sort of alienation, any distance between himself and the company for which he works. Hence the demand for permanent transformation, continuous improvement, which characterizes the process of self-development to which he is dedicated and which leads him to ceaselessly perfect his skills. From this point of view, the widespread use of the term "enterprise" is more than metaphorical, because it refers to all of an individual's activities, which are considered to be part of a continuous process of self-valorization. With neoliberalism, the evaluative dimension (part of the market economy since the beginning) was established in the form of "self-evaluation."

The personal investment at stake in this process is what in itself is transformed into capital, changing the role of work as much as that of consumption. Work is, shall we say, "liberated" from the passivity to which it was bound in its classical form. And, on the other hand, consumption becomes less and less confined to the simple activity of restoring lost strength, but itself an element of investment that enhances, increasing the very value of life. At stake are not so much specific work- or consumption-related activities, more or less easily quantifiable and, in this sense, possible to appropriate, but the element of potential intrinsic to human life, essential to the involvement of the "labor-power" within the production process since the beginning.[9] Today, this element unexpectedly takes center stage as "human capital": a "deposit" to be used in a process that, paradoxically, instead of enriching, impoverishes those same activities of which it takes advantage.

From this perspective, we could say that the methods by which economic power subjugates are in a way intrinsically connected to the same methods with which the subjects establish themselves, giving form and value to life. This process, internal to the economic context, is matched in the political context by another phenomenon essential for understanding what has happened in the last 40 years: the progressive transformation of national states into "Managerial States."

The total transformation of politics into economics, which has been widely discussed in recent years, did not happen only through the invasion and conquest – from the outside, so to speak – of states by a market that had become global. Rather, it was the same states, especially the stronger ones, that adopted the logic of the commercial enterprise and linked it to the market. The expansion of the financial market and the financing of public debt in the bond markets are two phenomena closely entwined and connected to another process of unprecedented dimensions that we have seen in recent years: the mass diversion of household savings into company shares. This development has led to the total involvement of individual lives in the financial world. In this way, private debt played a decisive role from the start of the global financial crisis that originated in the United States. The states were the protagonists in handling a managerial power that allowed them to transform themselves from "territorial states" into "business states." This transformation deeply affected the status of politics and the process of establishing rules.

It affected a range of practices internal to institutional and economic policies that also deeply affected individual lives, so much so that it radically transformed the boundaries between public and private, altering the configuration of politics. These conditions form the basis from which a genealogical study of the concept of debt is proposed here, with the intention of highlighting certain essential elements that have become prominent in recent years.

Genealogy of debt

In an early fragment entitled "Capitalism as Religion," Walter Benjamin – following up on the analysis presented by Friedrich Nietzsche in *On the Genealogy of Morality* – highlights, with great prophetic ability, the mechanism of infinite indebtedness at the core of the capitalist economy.[10] The connection between "debt" and "guilt" – implicit in the German word *Schuld/Schulden*, which covers both meanings – is central to this discussion.

In defining capitalism as an essentially religious phenomenon, Benjamin refers to the opening lines of Max Weber's well-known work on the capitalist economy's origin in Protestant asceticism.[11] According to Weber, the dominion of the capitalist economy is based on the intimate link that economic power establishes with individual forms of life. The "accounting" of existence implicit in the methodical control of ascetic practice means that "the sanctification of life" could "almost assume the character of a business," whose success is in itself a sign of approval.[12] The same mechanism, Weber argues, lies at the basis of the capitalist enterprise, which (significantly for our discussion) is the main subject of his analysis. Weber was, in fact, one of the first to emphasize the centrality of the enterprise and the figure of the entrepreneur in the dominance of the capitalist economy, in a sense predicting the developments we have seen in recent decades with the hegemony of the figure of the "entrepreneur of himself."

However, in the excerpt mentioned above, Benjamin criticizes Weber. In fact, he claims that the relationship between capitalism and religion relates not only to the historic development of secularization which, according to him, would emerge from the Weberian approach – that is to say, from the progressive and general detachment of other spheres of life from the religious sphere. Instead, he argues that the relationship implies a deeper connection, whose origin should be studied in entirely different terms. According to Benjamin, it cannot be only "Calvinism" that is involved here, as Weber argued, but rather Christianity as a whole. This is because, as Benjamin argues in the excerpt, "capitalism has developed as a parasite of Christianity in the West [...], until it reached the point where Christianity's history is essentially that of its parasite – that is to say, of capitalism."[13]

Benjamin therefore identifies a direct "parasitic" derivation of capitalism from Christianity, which in a way expands the dimension outlined by Weber, while cleansing it, however, of its linear historical development. Instead, a shared genealogical origin emerges between the two phenomena, which in my view makes Benjamin's approach extremely similar to the one proposed by Michel Foucault during the courses at the Collège de France in the late 1970s, which have become famous because it was there that neoliberalism was considered for the first time not only as an economic theory but as a new form of domination and political establishment.[14]

Consistently with the genealogical method used by Benjamin, Foucault also identifies a link between economic power (fundamentally intense as a form of government, as "governmental power") and Christianity, but not as simply a historically preexisting, foundational fact. More than the diachronic evolution of one from the other, the relationship between economy and Christianity rests upon a synchronic mechanism in which the device that feeds both of them is what matters. We could say that according to Foucault, what counts in their relationship is, as Benjamin puts it, the direct "parasitic" derivation and not the continuous historic development.

In 1978, during the "Security, Territory and Population"[15] course, while trying to define the concepts of "governmentality" and "governmental power" – essential for understanding the dominance of neoliberalism (as we also see in his subsequent course, published under the title *The Birth of Biopolitics*[16]) – Foucault identifies the specific device needed to clarify his theory in "Christian pastoral power." For Foucault, the power, which developed between the third and the eighteenth centuries, served as a premise for the production of new forms of governmentality in modern times, reactivated specifically in neoliberal forms of government. The power of the shepherd in Christianity is essentially that of taking responsibility for the lives of the flock, not only as a whole but also for each individual member (*"omnes et singulatim"*). It is a power that is not limited to imposing obedience through force but which customizes itself and is capable of reforming and guiding consciences. An inclusive reform of individuals and the collective is intimately related to the taking over of life that characterizes economic-governmental power.

In particular, neoliberalism, according to Foucault, made explicit a premise that had been implicit in capitalism since its origins: the fact that it was a complex "economic-institutional" system.[17] The institutional sphere, instead of deriving from an "ideological super-structure" that obstructs or favors the economic context, is an integral part of that system, so much so that it constitutes it from within. This process reproduces the same mechanism originally at work in the experience of

Christian life.

Following the path opened up by Foucault, we can in fact identify a new political institution present in Christianity since its beginnings. The word *oikonomía*, which in the Greek and Roman world referred to "government" and "administration" (*nómos*) of the home (*oîkos*) and was entirely distinct from the public and political activity of the city (*pólis*), in Christianity defines the administrative realm of faith in Christ. This is the activity entrusted to those participating in the new constitution of the Church as a religious and at the same time political community. It is here that for the first time the economy becomes political and politics transforms itself into a new field of rule-making, starting with the administrative management of the community.

On this basis, we can see why, according to Foucault, Christianity is the invention of a power that is obliging but not extrinsically coercive, in which single subjects are individually and collectively involved (*omnes et singulatim*) precisely because they are free. That is to say, in the experience of life in Christ, the more one is free and relieved of an ultimately extrinsic bond of obligation to the Law, the more one is obedient on the basis of a relationship of absolute adjustment of life to the Law.

It is particularly interesting in this context to note that the word used in the New Testament to discuss "sin" is actually "debt," as we see clearly in the Greek version of the well-known gospel verses of Matthew (Mt. 6 and 12), later incorporated into the famous The Lord's Prayer: "Forgive us our debts (*opheílema*) as we forgive our debtors." As New Testament scholar Raymond Brown has pointed out, "in secular Greek there is no religious connotation" for the word *opheílema*, which appears in the gospel and translates the Aramaic *hôbâ* ("debt").[18] This means that for a Greek living at that time, the New Testament vocabulary used to indicate sin had a meaning related to economics.[19]

The Jewish experience of "guilt" as "sin," on which Christian life is also based, fully becomes an experience of a "debt" that, through the gift of "grace," is not merely repaid but as such is managed in faith in Christ, because it is here that an investment is possible. The economic administration of faith does not, in this sense, contradict the munificent gratuitousness from which it derives, but both are connected to the experience of a radical insolvency that must not be amended, because that is what generates profit. From this perspective, exploiting life is an investment, which, in the view of Paul the Apostle, cannot be realized in "deeds," which are incapable of fulfilling the precepts of the Law, so that the state of guilt and condemnation, in which human life finds itself, is radically laid bare. Only faith in Christ makes it possible for the debt incurred to be transformed into a "deposit" to be managed. The price of redemption paid by Christ, in fact, freely justifies those who have faith, establishing the economic management of a gift, which does not require the obligation of compensation or genuine sacrificial activity.

Paolo Napoli, a scholar of Michel Foucault and the history of normative apparatuses, rightly sees in the "deposit of faith in Christ" – extensively discussed in *Lettere Pastorali* – a real "juridical institution," in which not only "the depositor (creditor) delivers a mobile good to the depositary (debtor) who agrees to store and return it at the request of the former,"[20] but which also unites "the administrative requirement – the depositary is the holder and not the owner of the good – to a spreading trend [...] of faith."[21] In this sense, "the deposit of faith" is ultimately "an inheritance that does not tolerate appropriation and asks only to be safeguarded."[22]

Thus, at stake in the apparatus of the "deposit of faith" is "a protective approach,"[23] in which Paolo Napoli identifies "a deontological constant" which in some way "links the Apostle Paul to any financial adviser of our times: receiving a deposit means managing it," he explains.[24] We can understand, therefore, how the original capital, that is the deposit, represents the engine of an enterprise that consists of transforming a faith in the church[25] – of transforming, we could say, an act of faith into an act of politics. With regard to the origin of the constitution of the Christian church itself, Napoli's words, "the deposit appears as the normative archetype for formulating the birth and operation of an administrative institution on a global scale."[26]

But "if the deposit presumes an economy, it is not one of exchange, but rather of managerial efficiency, of government."[27] This implies that it is possible to identify in the first Christian community the prototype of an economic-administrative institution, in which the normative sphere is not defined exclusively on the basis of an obliging constraint but also on that of a "remedy." "The remedy of the deposit and the deposit as a remedy" is at the core of an apparatus that celebrates "administrative praxis as the supreme salvific cause."[28]

This passage not only sheds light on the link between "Christian pastoral power" and "governmental power" as identified by Foucault and widely discussed[29]; it also helps us understand the mechanism currently at work in the governance of global indebtedness, which does not seem to contradict Foucault's analysis but instead has radicalized the same premises. Debt is not so much, or not only, a condition to be amended – as the authoritarian order for sacrifice imposed through austerity policies would seem to imply – or a legal constraint that submits to an infinite commitment, but more a condition in which to invest, even through regeneration policies, for an economy fundamentally structured on the basis of an administrative institutional logic.

The reunification of Germany and the European crisis: examples of fiduciary administration

After the Second World War, when Germany found itself faced with the task of reconstructing a nation that was by then internally divided and occupied, it was compelled to break ties with the devastation caused by its recent history. To gain credibility with its citizens, it could not reclaim legal legitimacy in the first instance, because despite the violation of all rights this had never been fully withdrawn even with the national-socialist state – hence the large problem of the responsibility of the Germans on the one hand and the question of the legal status of the provisions made during Nazism on the other hand.

It was ultimately a question of needing to invent a new institution capable of producing legitimacy and consent from the void of legitimization left by the trauma of recent history. It was the guarantee of the exercise of economic liberty that provided the legitimizing foundation for a new state, which rose up as a result of an enormous collective effort born of the urgency of processing an overwhelming loss and the simultaneous need to radically neglect history.[30]

It was Ludwig Erhard, the Christian Democrat member of parliament and economics minister for West Germany for 14 consecutive years after the fall of the Nazi regime and the father of the "German economic miracle," who found a legitimizing basis for the state in the exercise of economic freedom. A process that happened thanks to the formulation of the "social market economy" development model, which resulted in the famous "third way" – a political-economic configuration which on the one hand originated in the economic theories of the Freiburg School's ordoliberalism, but which is also and essentially characterized by a strong Christian influence that has yet to be explored, especially in relation to the influence that western Germany has exercised over Europe since the end of the war.

It is no coincidence, for example, that among the key theorists of the post-war German economic administration was the Jesuit theologian Oswald von Nell-Breuning, former adviser to Pope Pius XI and author, among other works, of the interesting article *Neoliberismus und katholische Soziallehre*[31] (1955). Well known, in fact, is his collaboration in the writing of the encyclical *Quatragesimo Anno*, in which the validity of the social doctrine of the Catholic church is reaffirmed in line with the *Rerum Novarum* of 1891.

It is a little-studied chapter of contemporary history, which has enormous consequences not only for Germany but also for its role in the formation and recent developments of the European Union. From this perspective, for example, the recent European crisis would not be considered so much as a failure of politics in relation to the dominance of the Common Market economy. Rather, the European Union, following in the footsteps of Germany, emerged as a political institution on the basis of the same market freedom on which the German Federal Republic was built after the war. In both cases, it was economic freedom that produced political legitimation, through the consent of all those agents on the inside of the economic process. This consent is beginning to show its most critical aspects, even though within it there do not appear to be any alternative options that could truly be feasible. The return to sovereignist positions contrary to European policies, more than being an alternative, in fact seems to be the symptom of a deeper unease.

To better understand what happened and to find a different approach to the situation we are still facing, it may be useful to remember how in 2011, in the midst of the Greek crisis, the then head of the Eurogroup (and President of the European Commission) Jean-Claude Juncker, in an interview published in *Der Spiegel*, made explicit reference to the model adopted during the reunification of Germany as an example to be followed in Greece: the *Treuhandanstalt*, or "Trust Agency," the protagonist of the 1990-1994 reunification process.[32]

With regard to this subject, we usually reference the massive and extremely rapid process of privatizing the economy of the German Democratic Republic. In reality, on closer inspection, the transformation was more subtle. The privatization of state-owned companies was not, in fact, among the original objectives of the *Treuhandanstalt*; instead, there was the aim of reorganizing and protecting public property in the context of social relationships and capitalist production. The idea was to create "a trust agency for the protection of the nation's patrimony," whose purpose was certainly to privatize the Democratic Republic's assets, but done in a manner akin to management of an inheritance on behalf of a trustee. Essentially, the new agency functioned as a trust fund – using the model of the "deposit of faith in Christ" discussed earlier – into which all the Democratic Republic's assets were conferred, to increase the capacity for development and the possibility of attracting new investments, including and primarily from foreigners (specifically those from western Germany).

We cannot review here the complex vicissitudes of this process; its results, however, became evident to everyone.[33] The extension of the Deutsche Mark's domain to eastern Germany was the definitive event that in fact created the political unity of Germany. The citizens of the former Democratic Republic were initially enthusiastic about this development, which for them essentially meant sharing in the well-being enjoyed in the West. Consequently, the Christian Democrat Kohl and his allies in the East won the 1990 elections in a landslide victory. However, the problems associated with conferring the public patrimony of the Democratic Republic to the *Treuhandanstalt* in exchange for the "gift" of the Deutsche Mark soon became clear. This decision was perhaps not given due consideration (probably not by coincidence) at the time when Europe decided to move from national currencies to the euro.

In any event, in light of everything that happened, it was incredible to see, in 2011, Jean-Claude Juncker turning to the *Treuhandanstalt* to resolve the crisis in Greece. The "*Treuhandanstalt* model*" was implemented again and subsequently proposed by prominent representatives from the fields of economics and politics, including Frank-Walter Steinmeier, then leader of the Social Democrats (SPD) in the Bundestag, foreign minister during the coalition governments of Angela Merkel, and today president of the Federal Republic of Germany. In an interview with the *Rheinische Post*, Steinmeier argued, "It is absolutely worth considering the idea of a European model of *Treuhand* into which the national patrimony of Greece would be placed. This *Treuhand* can privatize it in 10 or 15 years. With the revenue, Greece could reduce its debt and finance investments in development."[34] In essence, this was another way of saying what Angela Merkel had already stated: Greece too must accept that it has to make the necessary sacrifices. Ultimately, even Germany had to face a structural transformation, which for the former GDR meant tough, but indispensable reforms.[35]

The austerity programs linked to the public debt negotiations were accompanied by the reforms requested by Europe – the real "exchange goods" in this process – which were passively accepted by the governments of some indebted European countries such as Italy, Spain, Portugal and Ireland but, at least initially, bitterly opposed by Greece. At stake in the negotiations, in fact, was not so much, or not only, the full payment of the debt but rather the same neoliberal policies that affect individual lives in an unprecedented manner and are therefore the real condition for a possible restructuring of the debt.

If in neoliberalism the evaluative dimension was imposed in the form of a "self-evaluation" of one's individual capacities, then fundamentally involved in neoliberal reforms are the same individual capabilities, in themselves potentially open, but transformed at the root, until one starts to suffer the frustration of never feeling adequate for the situation presented. There is a constant self-criticism at the core of a continuous sense of guilt, of which the fundamental characteristic is that it originates in an (economic) form of evaluation: that is, in the possibility of investing in a lack, which is ultimately an indebting condition. An infinite debt is thus reproduced, which materially comes from obsessive forms of consumption, which is intended to compensate for a conviction that one is never able to meet expectations. At a closer look, however, what is at stake is a "debt of life" which feeds on those same capabilities that are exploited precisely in the degree that they are continuously devalued.

Restoring opportunity to what currently tends to establish itself as only a lack is therefore what we must consider in order to change the conditions of what seems to be just a web with no way out. This restoration of opportunity is connected to the difficult task of finding a political response to the self-destructive form that the global enterprise we are witnessing has now assumed. In this context, even the revived power of religion in the global public arena perhaps becomes more understandable. We could perhaps hypothesize that the various fundamentalist belief systems that have recently emerged and developed, such as that of the ISIS jihadis, are closely linked to the hegemony of global economic power, precisely because this too derives its efficacy from being a fundamentally religious apparatus. The Islamization of radicalism that has taken shape among the younger generations in our opulent metropolises and the "social market economy" are essentially nothing more than two sides of the same complex phenomenon, which we cannot excuse ourselves from addressing if we are to find new ways of living together and different things in which to believe.

Translated by Arianna Bove.

7. Interview with Mark Blyth

Arjen Kleinherenbrink

Mark Blyth is a British political scientist and a professor of international political economy at Brown University. Drawing on political science, economics, sociology and complexity theory, his research concerns the politics of ideas, institutional change, and the politics of finance. His recent works include *Austerity: The History of a Dangerous Idea* (2012) and *The Future of the Euro* (2015, co-edited with Matthias Matthijs).

Arjen Kleinherenbrink: I'd like to start by asking you about your perspective on the 2008 financial crisis. In Austerity – The History of a Dangerous Idea, *you argue that the tendency to refer to it as a sovereign debt crisis is "the greatest bait and switch in modern history." What, then, was the* real *crisis, and why has it been misconstrued as a sovereign debt crisis?*

Mark Blyth: It really was a private debt crisis, which was covered up because we had already bailed the banks out once before. In 2008, there had already been a series of bailouts (Northern Rock in the UK, Hypo Real Estate in Germany, Fortis in Belgium, ING in the Netherlands and so on). So, the public had already been told once, "Look, this is terrible and we really should not be bailing out these banks, because they took terrible risks...but that is just the way it is."

This all started with the 2007 subprime mortgage crisis in the United States, which somewhat unexpectedly turned out to have all sorts of channels into Europe. European banks and financial institutions had set up special investment funds to buy up large quantities of dodgy American mortgages, meaning that the balance sheet risk of those assets was transferred to Europe. In addition to purchasing impaired mortgages, those institutions had also bought up a lot of debt from peripheral European economies. So, what happened when it became apparent that the global recession was going to impact Europe? Those assets rapidly began to lose value. And remember that these banks were massively leveraged, meaning that they only had a tiny capital cushion. Deutsche Bank, for example, was running 66 to 1 leverage on an average Tuesday in 2008. If you then lose 3 percent of your assets, you are not just illiquid, you are insolvent!

This is where the sovereign debt crisis became important. With banks in such weak capital positions, a Greek default would have dragged down every single one of them. To cover their losses on Greece, banks would start to sell Irish assets, causing their value to fall to zero. The same thing would happen to Portuguese assets. But then you get to Spain and Italy, which are in a sense too big to sell. So, you would have had a bank run going through the bond markets of Europe, and that is what all those yields going up were. This then forces you to step in and suppress those yields in order to keep things somewhat safe. How can you do that? First, you try austerity. You convince the markets that slashing state budgets will make deficits go down and prevent further debt growth. The only problem was that everybody was trying this at the same time, causing the denominator – the size of the economy – to shrink. And that effectively meant that the same amount of debt got bigger, not smaller. Just look at what happened to Greece and Portugal. They implemented austerity measures, but debts increased because their economies got smaller. So, austerity does not work. The second option is what Mario Draghi then did: taking central bank action with cheap money and starting to buy up assets, which turned out to be effective.

So, what have we done? We really took a private sector crisis of leverage and put it on the public balance sheet, either through austerity or through central bank action. But we called it a sovereign debt crisis because we had *already* bailed out the banks, and we could not go back to the public and tell people that they were effectively bailing out the banks *twice*.

AK: If private debt was at the root of the previous financial crisis, are we now – 10 years later – in a "better" position when it comes to private debt (if we look at stagnation in real wages, credit card culture and so on)? Or are we simply heading for a repetition of past mistakes?

MB: Well, circumstances change and you cannot expect history to simply repeat itself. But has the credit position of the private sector gotten any better? Not really. We are again building massive asset and credit bubbles, which is an unintended consequence of saving these assets the first time around. By buying up these assets, chasing yield suppression (the ECB's current policy) and pushing down interest rates, money becomes cheap. This inevitably encourages another upswing in the credit cycle.

But at the same time, we have got a cyclical upturn in Europe, which everybody is hoping will continue. We are seeing the beginning of real wage growth, plus even some employment growth in the economies of southern Europe. If you have wage growth, less of people's take-home wages would go toward the servicing of debt. That could even reduce pressures for populism, because it would be a form of redistribution. So, right now there is a lot of focus on how we get those wages up. It is not entirely clear how you can do that in a globalized economy that is undergoing massive technological change. You can, for example, try to shut down tax havens and you can try to go after large multinationals. But redistribution from the 0.1 percent, particularly in the corporate sector, is inherently difficult. It is a multilateral effort that requires everybody to be on the same team. Admittedly, the EU has been making some interesting moves with regards to this. So, you can definitely redistribute and help people *revolve* these credit issues (as opposed to fixed payments), but I am not completely sure if we are in a world where you ever get to a point of *resolving* those credit issues.

AK: Now that you have mentioned the – thorny – issue of getting multinationals to pay their taxes, what is your take on the recent publication of the Paradise Papers? The Panama Papers seemed to cause massive (popular) outrage, but the lack of such outcries concerning the Paradise Papers almost seems to suggest that we have simply accepted that the world's ultra-rich are really somewhat like cartoon villains with secret lairs and vaults hidden away somewhere...

MB: People cannot be outraged all the time. There is a decay function on outrage. But I don't really agree that there is this acceptance. Take, for example, the statement of intent signed by the European finance ministers that effectively put these persons and entities on warning. In addition, try to take an investor's point of view on the fact that we now know that Apple literally pays *no* taxes, which suggests that it makes money through nothing more than tax avoidance. Once you are aware of such a huge vulnerability, why should anyone continue to invest in Apple equities? So, there *is* a way in which the system will have to reconfigure, and there will be some kind of reckoning on taxes. In the United States, you see something similar in terms of anti-trust regulation. For example, Amazon will become the first trillion-dollar company, and then it will be broken up. That is when you get to tax the different fragments. These are examples of redistribution-in-the-works. I am quietly hopeful that as long as the cyclical upturn lasts, pressure will move toward corporations to actually give something back. How much is what remains to be seen.

AK: You have repeatedly argued for two alternatives to austerity politics. One of them is better and more effective taxation, especially concerning the type of entities that you have just talked about. The other is financial repression. Could you elaborate on what that would imply?

MB: When I started writing about financial repression, it turned out that Draghi was already ahead of me. Draghi's policy is effectively financial repression. What does that mean? You get local banks in peripheral EU economies to purchase large quantities of local bonds with all the super cheap money you have handed out, called LTROs. In public, you call this the "dangerous sovereign bank nexus," because it means that when the sovereign goes down, it drags down the local banks, and vice versa. But what you have then effectively done is create a captive audience. You have gotten them to buy all these local bonds, and you are the one who gets to set the yield. You get to set the pay-out. In a sense, that gives you control. It allows you to push down interest rates, which is exactly what happened in the periphery. This means that credit starts flowing again, because the central bank is finally doing what it is meant to do.

The limit to this strategy is that you cannot solve all fiscal problems with a single monetary tool, even if you are trying very hard. Take Italy, for example, where the problem is intimately tied up with demographic trends, a lack of investment, a lack of coherent industrial strategies, and other factors that their parliament will have to address. There is only so much that Draghi can do through interest rates and bond buying. This more or less starts kicking responsibilities back to governments, who, before the crisis, had basically given up any sense of being responsible. Politicians had effectively given up on the hard problems of regional policy: what to do about increasing socio-economic misery in rural areas, what to do about massive deskilling in some parts of the country and massive concentrations of wealth in the capitals, and so on? Even the crisis has not fully thrown that responsibility back to politicians yet.

We are no longer doing austerity, which is why we are growing. We *are* doing financial repression, but it has its limits. But there are also other things that you can do. Let's take a United States example. Compared to 1990, college tuition has gone up about 180 percent, state healthcare about 130 percent, childcare about 100 percent and real wages have barely increased. Imagine that you are a single mother. How much of your post-tax income do you have to spend just to put your kid in school? It's insane, right? Now, imagine that you could take Germany's public *KiTa* kindergarten system, and have a version of that for the United States. That would be the equivalent of giving that woman a 30 percent real wage hike. That shows how you can realize redistribution through the socialization of costs, rather than the redirection of income. You could fund it through general taxation, so that everybody pays a little bit more. But on a wealth of 17 trillion, how much does it cost to get some kindergarten places? Not that much. The real obstacle is that we have a politics – as you can now see with Trump and his tax reform – driven by a 0.1 percent that *really* wants to have everything, and they are not in the mood to give anything back.

AK: Now that you have mentioned him: you are – for better or worse – somewhat famous for introducing the term "Global Trumpism." You have argued that Trump's presidency is not a random occurrence, but part of a global pattern of events. Interestingly, you also think that contemporary right- as well as left-wing populism are manifestations of that same pattern. What exactly is this pattern?

MB: Imagine that capitalism is a computer, and it has its various bits of hardware. You can reconfigure that hardware to have a German, French or Swedish version of capitalism, but all these versions are ultimately highly similar. They all have capital markets, stock markets, comparable labor markets and so on. From the 1940s until the 1970s, the software written on that hardware was aimed at domestic expansion and full employment. The problem with that is that there was a flaw in the software, a flaw that the economist Michał Kalecki already identified in the 1940s. If you run labor markets at full employment for 30 years, they overheat. As long as you can restrict capital flows, businesses have to invest at home, which forces them to enhance productivity to stay profitable. Ultimately, this will generate inflation. And once inflation is above the level of the real rate of return for businesses, they stop investing. When they stop investing, you end with stagflation: the combination of unemployment and high inflation. So, the software for this economic "regime" blew up in a crisis of inflation. The software reset consisted in Reagan, Thatcher, institutionally independent central banks, the globalization of labor markets, et cetera. The problem with *that* is that it also liberated finance at a moment when both real interest rates and the demand for credit were high. So, as you then globalize and integrate, what happens? Interest rates will go down and then keep going down. How can you then still make money? By increasing the volume, which is precisely why Deutsche Bank ends up with 66 to 1 leverage on an average Tuesday.

This makes for an incredibly tightly coupled, but very fragile system, which went into full-blown crisis in 2008. In Europe, this was followed by a 10-year recession, because the crisis was handled badly. Now, you already *had* populist parties that had been around for a long time in Europe. Think of the National Front in France, the Progress Party in Norway, the Freedom Party in Austria and so on. And they already had issues that they were capitalizing on: immigration, religion, et cetera. But the crisis turbocharged populist parties. For the ones on the Left, they saw the private sector being bailed out and the public sector bearing the cost. For the ones on the Right, they saw a bunch of liberal elites who basically no longer care about their own nationals.

Incidentally, the surge of the populist Left has been the

real transformative effect, even though we all tend to focus on the Right, because it tends to generate the most noise. Think about the utter transformation of the Spanish party system, the Portuguese left-wing coalition, the center-left coalition in Romania, or about M5S now being the biggest Italian party. In terms of party systems, it is the Left that has brought about real transformations. Also look at Merkel in Germany: she was reelected with the lowest vote-share her party has ever had (and the SPD might just as well go into retirement). In the meanwhile, who is winning? We all focus on the AfD, but if you add together Die Linke and the Greens, their vote-share is higher than the AfD's. In any case, everywhere the "tails" of the political spectrum are where the action is, which manifests as both Left and Right populism. It all results from a very long-run process of the collapse of one growth regime, followed by the pathologies of the subsequent neoliberal regime.

AK: In a 2016 piece in Foreign Affairs that you wrote about this, the last sentence is "the era of neoliberalism is over, the era of neonationalism has just begun." Do you still stand by that, and what is this new era going to look like?

MB: My point is that, in a sense, the nation is the default container for anxiety. Economic processes may be global, but you do not experience the effects of something like Chinese trade directly, right? Income losses in your country or community might have something to do with Chinese trade (see David Autor's *The China Shock*), but that is not how you experience things. And politics is precisely about that local experience. So, you have a situation in which somebody turns up, one election cycle after the other, and they say "Vote for me for jobs, vote for me for hope, vote for me for change!" – but in the meanwhile your community slowly gets worse and worse. After a while, those politicians lose credibility. This is what happened to the center parties. And the people who *are* paying attention to those communities are in the tails on the Left and Right. What this means is: people vote locally, their welfare concerns are essentially national, and this leads to a nationalism. That could be a repressive nationalism, or a far more accepting and cosmopolitan one. But one thing that the populist Left and Right both grasp is that the nation is the economic unit, and that nationals are in need of some form of protection. How such protection is *defined* differentiates them, but ultimately, they are both about domestic protection against globalizing forces.

AK: One force that these populist parties frequently criticize is the euro and its concomitant monetary union. You have also called the euro a "monetary doomsday device"...could you explain why?

MB: When you join the euro and give up your own currency, you become a small part of a larger entity that financial markets effectively treat as a single country. There is an appealing aspect to this. The Eurozone is the richest part of the global economy, bigger than the United States. It is also really hard to short the euro, which basically means that you have a powerful central bank that can set prices – all of which is good. But from the point of view of local control, there are serious problems. The Greeks, for example, cannot devalue. And they cannot default, because the EU simply will not let them. Given how the global economy works, it is not entirely sure if the ability to devalue would actually give you control over your economy, but there is at the very least a perception that you have lost these tools, and that you have given up to these unelected EU bureaucrats. Again, that is something that populism is successfully tapping into, mostly because it directly resonates with people's lived experiences. So if you design a system where the default in a crisis is a form of adjustment where the weakest continually bear most of the costs, eventually it will break. In that sense it's a monetary doomsday device.

AK: The German sociologist Wolfgang Streeck has proposed to reintroduce national European currencies in addition to a euro (which would function as an overarching currency). Do you see any merit to that proposal?

MB: The problem is: when is the right time to do it? Do you try it during a crisis, when the markets are already freaked out? Or do you try it when things are going well...meaning that everybody will try to position themselves to get as much money as possible from the trade, which makes the whole move inherently unstable and difficult. So, the question is whether the markets will allow for it, *and* whether there is sufficient political will and imagination to do it. To me, the real constraint is that, basically, the political classes everywhere are horribly weak at the moment. I occasionally test this hypothesis at conferences with people from the financial sector. Note that these will be the kind of people who actively contribute to political campaigns and the funding of politicians. So, I will ask them: how many of you would hire the politicians that you fund to run a trading book in your firm? The response just tends to be embarrassed laughter. And this is painful: they will hire these politicians to run the country, but they would never hire them to run their own money. That tells you a lot about what they think about the quality of the governing classes.

AK:...does that mean that we will just get to watch the euro die a slow and possibly painful death?

MB: No, I do not think that will happen. My argument in *The Future of the Euro* is that there is a massive standing interest in maintaining the euro, even though the composition of the monetary union could change drastically (one could imagine a

North-South split of the type that Joseph Stiglitz has been talking about). At the end of the day, the biggest European economy is Germany, and a large number of (Eastern) European countries are part of the German supply chain. The interesting thing about Eastern European countries is that a lot of them talk a good game of joining the euro, but very few are actually doing it. They like to have the kind of control that comes with having your own currency. But what they essentially do with those currencies is shadow the euro. They are basically importing German levels of inflation and taking their cues from the ECB, because as long as Germany is selling BMWs to the rest of the world, it is great to make the transmissions and the software in Romania. So, these countries have a huge interest in maintaining the euro if only to shadow it.

On the other hand, say that you live in the south of Europe and Beppe Grillo gets a majority in an election and his first point of action is to organize a referendum about the euro. When that happens, every Italian citizen with a bank account in euros will try to open a bank account in Germany. Because if there is going to be a new lira, you can guarantee that it will be worth less than the euro. So, if I have savings, would I rather have German euros or Italian lira? And since everybody will ask themselves this question more or less at the same time, there will be a nationwide bank run. The Germans would then have to sterilize the flows by putting up capital controls, and that will be the end of the euro.

In other words, even though the whole thing is very fragile, there is still a lot of interest, particularly with the exporters in the North, in keeping this thing going. Let me also stress that it is not even clear to what extent going back to a national currency actually gives you real control over your interest rates, because you will be a relatively small country that will then be exposed to a globalized world.

AK: I'd like to move to a slightly different topic. In Austerity, *you also entertain the notion that the end of financialization may be nigh, which is not something that you hear every day. What did you mean by that?*

MB: Well, what I meant was that there has been a one-time period from 1980 to 2008 when real interest rates were unprecedentedly high. You could walk into a Citibank in the United States in 1991 (well, Chemical Bank as they were then) and get nearly double figures for opening a savings account. That time is gone. The long-run real rate of interest for the global economy is 2 percent, and inflation is also around 2 percent. Everything is long and low, and central banks are pushing yields down...and keeping them down. That makes it harder to make money in finance. The City of London has lost 50,000 jobs since the financial crisis. As a sector, the financial industry is shrinking. Its value may be stable, but employment is on the decline. And then there is "Fintech": financial technology. Fintech 1.0 will replace the entire back office, which is about 60 percent of people working in the industry. We are already at the point where algorithms and robots take care of 40 percent of global equity trading. Fintech 2.0 (augmented intelligence, deep machine learning and so on) will see machines making the vast majority of the trades. Does it then still matter where these companies are located, particularly if they are not creating any jobs? And by the way, robots and automation are not the problem. We need robots, because we are getting older and because we need productivity enhancements. Financialization as a set of processes and practices will continue, but it will change in content so much that what we recognize today as financialization will disappear.

AK: But we tend to resist the automation of work, partly because we value work for the sake of working itself...

MB: Which brings us to the debate on universal basic income.

I really think there is something to the argument that work is about more than just doing a job. The notion that you would have millions of unemployed European adults sitting at home and playing guitar...I think that may very well turn out to be a nightmarish fantasy. Your identity comes from your work, your social network comes from your work, and your sense of self-worth comes from your work. From studies on the effects of long-term unemployment, even in societies with good labor market protections and welfare structures, we know that it correlates with collapse in skill formation, lower lifetime earnings, higher rates of depression, higher rates of alcoholism and so on. That means there is a real downside to not working. On the other hand, some of the UBI experiments show that people become more public-minded, that they do not stop working and so on. This is why we need large-scale pilot studies to figure out if this works or not. Because *if* that is the outcome, it is brilliant. But I worry that the outcome will be some kind of Protestant nightmare whereby idleness and the devil's work really turn out to go together. So, I'm very much on the fence on this, and I need more evidence before I really make a claim as to how this works.

AK: Is work not also losing value, even if it is not threatened by automation? Not in the classical sense of hyper-specialization, but in terms of the increasing precariousness of labor and the increasing rarity of stable employment.

MB: Look at the American data from the 2016 Katz & Krueger Report ("The Rise and Nature of Alternative Work"). They find that 91 percent of all jobs created since 2008 are gig economy jobs. The interesting thing there is the bifurcation of wages. There are absolutely a ton of these jobs at the bottom (Deliveroo, Uber and so on). But there is also a good deal of them at the very top. It ultimately depends on where you are, which brings us to Branko Milanović's point that what determines inequality these days is geography more than anything else. If you are born into a middle-class family in a good school district in New York City, and you learn Python in high school, and you then go on to Columbia University, then you are going to be *fine*. But if you live in the Midwest and you do not have access to those networks and that knowledge, it is a very different story. In a way, geography becomes destiny in this world, particularly if it is tech-enhanced. I do not think governments have really begun to take this into consideration. If you look at the way that wealth gets concentrated, it is not just across income distribution, but also geographically. Wealth concentrates at the coasts and in the capital cities, while the hinterland is being hollowed out.

AK: While we are on the subject, can we get your view on how economic problems relating to precarious jobs, private debts and mounting inequality are intertwined with various forms of identity politics (whether of a progressive or a reactionary kind) in contemporary (populist) politics? For example, how is it that the fear and anger resulting from economic decline often manifests as antagonism between cultural groups?

MB: That's because of people's very real-life experiences. Take the German elections. You have a lot of communities in East Germany where there are no immigrants, but they are completely for the AfD. So, why is that? Well, these people have been living in communities where things have not been very good for a very long time. Young people are leaving in droves, incomes are shrinking and so on. Then, suddenly, your government decides: *Wir schaffen das!* We can do this! We can take a lot of new people in (migrants), give them language training, give them skills, put them in schools and integrate them into the labor market. Which makes you think: what about me, and what about my kids? So, immigration is felt incredibly differently across the income distribution. And the Left and the Right are just talking past each other on this point. The Left just wants to tell the Right that they are a bunch of racists, and the Right just wants to tell the Left that they are a bunch of cosmopolitans who do not care about normal/national people.

AK: As a final question, another point that you make in Austerity *is how we seem to collectively mistrust the state (and here, too, there is a Left as well as a Right version of this). Yet historically, the major periods of twentieth-century economic growth were characterized by relatively large governments, major public expenditures, sophisticated welfare structures and so on. Is this something that we ought to try to return to...and is such a thing even possible?*

MB: Well, it's not even as if we have ever really left that behind. If you look at the share of GDP spent by governments, it did not really decline. Part of the reason for this is public pensions and the vast increase in elderly citizens. The majority of the British welfare budget is now spent on pensioners, but of course, that is not what people pay attention to. Instead, the attention always goes to unemployed "cheats" who would "exploit" the welfare system. But pensions are really most of the expense. The big state has not gone away, it has just redirected most of its spending to pensions, instead of investing in R&D, green-tech, diffusing populism or reducing the costs for working families. They are basically in a maintenance mode of keeping people's debts from rolling over and stopping the system from blowing up, while at the same time trying to manage these Left and Right populist pressures.

This goes back to my fundamental point: I really believe that the quality of the capital and political classes across the world has declined to a point where their members are functionally unable to actually see what the problems are. Until we realize a change in those governing classes, we will not really see these problems brought to the agenda. All you will get is maintenance and management, which is the only thing these people are good at, and even then, good is a relative term.

8. Interview with Andrea Fumagalli

Arjen Kleinherenbrink

Andrea Fumagalli is a militant researcher and professor of economics in the Department of Economics and Management at the University of Pavia. His recent publications include *The Crisis of the Global Economy: Financial Markets, Social Struggles and New Political Scenarios* (2010, with Sandro Mezzadra) and *La vie mise au travail. Nouvelles forms du capitalisme cognitif* (2015). He is also an active member of the Basic Income Earth Network and the Basic Income Network, Italy.

Arjen Kleinherenbrink: In "A financial monetary economy of production," you and Stefano Lucarelli discuss how the principle novelty of post-Fordist capitalism is the creation of credit money sustained by household debt. Financial markets are at the heart of this new capitalism, and wage earners are increasingly asked to entrust money to their operators – directly as well as indirectly (via pension funds, et cetera). This clearly spiraled out of control and became one of the primary factors in the 2007-8 financial crisis. In your view, has there been any change to this situation in the years following the crisis? And what kind of policy measures or restraints would be needed to prevent renewed crises – if such measures are even possible?

Andrea Fumagalli: I will answer personally, without consulting Stefano. Financial markets are able to create virtual money via capital gains and debt induction. The counter effect of this situation is that we face structural instability due to the rise of speculative bubbles, these can burst if the decrease of wages and income polarization is not compensated by a financial multiplier on aggregate demand. Unfortunately, this is now normal. Therefore, a new crisis cannot be avoided, only postponed.

This situation did not change after the crisis. What has changed is the monetary policy (goodbye to the monetarist approach!), which is now more able to support the financial conventions and to ensure the necessary liquidity (quantitative easing). This kind of policy, in any case, is not able to give structural answers to the origin of the crisis. It's only a palliative measure. Financial markets, after 4 decades of expansion and concentration (unprecedented in 2 centuries of capitalism), are not reformable and their power is out of control.

If we consider that on the US derivatives market, four big financial enterprises control more than 95 percent of the correspondent flows, the present status of financial markets presents a market structure which hardly allows any attempt to make it more transparent. The degree of concentration in the different financial markets is so high that any limitation risks either being useless or causing more harm than good. So, this is not just "too big to fail," but also "too big to be controlled and reformed."

AK: You also discuss how the financial crisis stems from the euphoria of the 1990s, specifically from overinvestment in information and communication technologies, with a synergy existing between the creation of new financial instruments and technological innovation. Could you elaborate on the importance of this link, and on its relevance to problematics concerning credit money?

AF: The subprime crisis of 2008 can be interpreted as a crisis of a Finance Production system. This type of capitalist dynamics is going to substitute the traditional monetary production system as elaborated by Keynes in *A Treatise on Money* (1930). A Finance Production system is strictly correlated with the dynamics of technical change in different fields: financial innovations (derivatives, increases in money velocity, financial product innovations, change in the governance of financial markets toward a greater deregulation beginning in the 1980s and so on); production innovations (robotics, artificial intelligence, big data mining, space technologies, military innovations, logistics, transport, et cetera); life innovations (bio-technologies, wealth, pharmaceutical, genomes); communication innovations (social media, among others).

We are now witnessing an emerging technological paradigm based on the hybridization of humans with machines (the becoming machine of human) and of the machines with humans (the becoming human of machines) in which vital faculties, learning and network processes, experiences and human relationships in general are subjected to labor and to value-creation.

In this framework, financial markets play the role of financing all these activities by substituting in a complementary way the role played by credit money in the Fordist paradigm. From this point of view, financial markets are the engine and the fuel of the accumulation in a bio-cognitive valorization and they are not under any control by monetary institutions (which can only follow the "financial conventions" organized and supported by the large financial oligarchies – hierarchies now able to control international financial flows).

AK: In Crisis in the Global Economy, *you also note how, in official EU policy documents responding to the crisis, the necessity to prevent interventions from "politicizing" the regulation of (financial) markets is strongly emphasized. This suggests the belief that market failure is merely incidental, that the financial system as such is "healthy" in principle, and that political intervention in markets can only ever disturb the functioning of that system. What is your view on the sources of this reluctance? Where does it come from, and how can it be that the faith in the self-regulatory character of markets still seems (on the level of policy) to be largely intact after the 2007-2008 crisis?*

AF: The choice not to regulate financial markets is a political one, even if from an economic point of view such regulation was already almost impossible in 2009-10, because of the new role played by the same financial markets and of the enormous political and uncontrolled power concentrated in a few hands.

Political power today is a direct emanation of economic hierarchies, especially of financial ones (see Trump in the US). In that period, in Europe, the technocrats decided to cover the budget losses of the banking system, resorting to strong injections of public spending with the result being an increased public deficit. In Mediterranean countries, this situation was used to impose even stronger limits on public spending (austerity policies) in order to foster an economic policy based on increased indirect taxation (VAT), labor precarization and welfare dismantling (privatization and financialization of health and education systems). In theory, the excuse was the supposed efficiency of free markets as postulated by neo-liberalist doctrine, but the real aim was to protect the richer segments of society from the potential income stagnation resulting from the financial crisis. In this way, the political choice was to shift the burden of the crisis from the richest to the poorest classes.

I think that no serious economist or politician can believe in the stability of the free-market economy and its possibility to reach Pareto efficiency. Such a belief is simply merely convenient, from certain points of view...

AK: You have written (in "Twenty theses on contemporary capitalism") that no "new deal" is possible, that a (possibly Keynesian) reformist politics to guarantee financial and economic stability is only possible in theory but not in practice. Why is this the case?

AF: If the origin of the structural instability of bio-cognitive capitalism lies in the fact that financial markets are not always able to provide an increase of aggregate demand through the distorted financial multiplier (which, on the contrary, determines income polarization) and, from the supply side, in the fact that learning and network economies, at the basis of the process of accumulation, are not put in conditions to be fully exploited because of intellectual property rights and labor precarity, it follows that a reasonable compromise can be based on two radical measures: unconditional basic income and free access to knowledge (abolition of intellectual property rights, after the period necessary to repay the investment in R&D).

Unconditional basic income frees the people from the blackmail of need. The main reason behind the asymmetry in the capital/labor ratio which allows for exploitation (the necessity to work for a living) then disappears. Indirectly, a basic income (only if unconditional) is indirectly and potentially subversive and, hence, will not be accepted by the economic hierarchy, which strongly relies on the perceived "obliged" necessity to "freely" work to get an income. The abolition of intellectual property rights means the abolition of private property. A capitalist society is defined by the legal acknowledgment of private property and by the legal labor exchange based on the necessity to work. If these two conditions fail, we are in a non-capitalist society.

AK: In response to the 2007-8 crisis, many governments either voluntarily adopted or were pressured to implement austerity measures. In most cases, this meant an increased dismantling of social programs and welfare structures, so that "caretaker" functions previously warranted by the state became the responsibility of individuals. Simultaneously, as you and Cristina Morini argue in "Life put to work," it is precisely the affective (caring, emotional) component of labor that becomes ever more central in a post-Fordist mode of what you call "biocapitalism." What are the most important features of the intersection of these two trends? And what are some of the other main features of biocapitalism as opposed to previous iterations of capitalism?

AF: The aim of austerity policies is mainly twofold. First, to increase the private financialization of welfare provisions, such as wealth, education, social security and so on. Second, to insert welfare activity in the accumulation process. Actually, in bio-cognitive capitalism, welfare systems are a direct mode of production. They directly produce surplus value, particularly with regards to "social reproduction." This concept, as developed through the seminal contributions of Cristina Morini (starting with "The Feminization of Labour in Cognitive Capitalism", 2007), nowadays covers a wider range of activities which surpass the boundaries of traditional "care activity," and also involve the psychological and physical maintenance of life itself (body, mind, procreation, care and so on). It is not surprising that all these activities must be commodified in order to extract life-value, by exploiting unpaid or underpaid labor. They represent an enlargement of the basis of contemporary accumulation, a sort of primitive accumulation, in Marxist terms, whose sectors are today the ones with the highest added value per employee.

Bio-cognitive capitalism is based on the exploitation of all the different aspects of life, from free time to education, health, sentiments, sexuality, communications, social media, consumption and so on.

AK: Again in Crisis in the Global Economy, *you further argue that social governance is now tied to what you call a form of "blackmail" that feeds off an increasing precarization of labor. Could you explain what this blackmail consists in, both on the individual and collective scale?*

AF: Social governance is composed by different processes. The first is represented by the contemporary role of debt, which has increased significantly at the micro level during the crisis.

We refer not only to the national debt but, overall, to the rise of "indebted man" (Lazzarato), tied to and repressed by monetary constraints.

The second process of social governance is represented by the evolution of types of labor tending toward a structural, existential and generalized *condition of precarity*. The precarious condition today is synonymous with uncertainty, instability, nomadism, blackmail and psychological subordination in order to survive. It is a dependency condition that does not manifest itself at the very moment in which it formally defines a labor contract. Actually, it is not only a juridical situation, but rather a sociological and anthropological situation. It's an existential condition that induces total forms of self-control and self-repression with even stronger results than those of the direct discipline of the factory. The precarious condition defines an anthropology and behavioral psychology that becomes all the more salient as labor becomes more cognitive and relational.

Debt on the one hand and precarity on the other are the two main pillars that allow the current *life subsumption* of bio-cognitive capitalism to operate. These two main elements favor an individualization of economic and social behavior toward what Dardot and Laval call the "entrepreneurial man," a sort of a neoliberal anthropology that defines a new subjective regime, and which needs to be addressed.

AK: In that same volume, in the eighth from a series of ten theses on the financial crisis, you state that "the financial crisis highlights two internal contradictory principles of cognitive capitalism: the insufficiency of the traditional forms of labor remuneration and the vileness of the proprietary structure." Part of this contradiction is that the division between work and life is no longer well-defined, or even existent. In light of this thesis, could you elaborate on your advocacy for a basic income, and on how the implementation of a basic income could address some of the problems you detect in contemporary (financialized) capitalism?

AF: Basic income should be considered the remuneration of that part of life that takes part in the valorization process without being acknowledged as a labor activity (and therefore not remunerated). From this point of view, basic income is a "primary income" and plays the same role as wages, which remunerate certified labor time as such; or profit, that rewards business activity; or rent, which derives from a property right. To understand why basic income is a "primary income" and not a simple income aid (as traditionally intended in the Fordist context), it is necessary to analyze the main sources of exploitation/valorization in contemporary capitalism. More and more studies and case studies confirm that today life itself, in all daily events, is the productive factor *par excellence*. If we take into account the acts of daily life that characterize our existence, they can be divided into four types: labor, work, leisure, and entertainment / games. The time of creation (*opus/ work*), the *otium*/leisure time, entertainment time: all are included in a growing and continuous valorization mechanism. The classic dichotomy of the Fordist paradigm between labor and non-labor time, between production and consumption, between production and reproduction is now partially obsolete. It is the result of a historical process of structural changes in manufacturing processes and labor organization, which marked the transition from a material Fordist capitalism to a bio-cognitive and financialized capitalism. Today, wealth production simultaneously derives from absolute surplus value and relative surplus value extraction, where for absolute surplus value we mean the existence of a sort of primitive accumulation in capitalist organizations that is based on capital employment and on private property. The result is a change of the relationship between productive and unproductive labor. What in material Fordist capitalism was considered unproductive (i.e.

not producing surplus value and therefore not remunerable), has now become productive, while remuneration nonetheless remains anchored to the Fordist era (salarization crisis).

It follows that basic income as remuneration must be unconditional. It guarantees income continuity, and not only the right to work but the right to choose the work one does. Therefore, it gives us the possibility to say "no" to the necessity of work for life. From this point of view, it is one useful tool among others (minimum wage, for instance), to reduce the blackmail of precarity and to have the freedom of self-determination and autonomy. And this, as I have already said, is potentially subversive.

AK: Yet some would argue that a basic income would only make individuals "lazy," making them spend most of their time on "unproductive" leisure activities that would apparently have no added value to society. Quite often, this argument goes hand-in-hand with the assertion that governments should instead strive for full employment. What would your response to such arguments be?

AF: This objection is entirely nonsensical, since we are all productive. The real distinction does not lie between employed and unemployed people, but between who is remunerated and who is not. The increasing share of unpaid labor confirms this trend. Secondly, I personally do not believe that it is human nature to be lazy. Quite the opposite: it is human nature to be active, if, of course, such activity can result from a free choice and matches the expectations, characteristics and desires of human beings. As Dante wrote: "You were not born to live as brutes, but to follow virtue and knowledge."

AK: Finally, in the third of your "Twenty theses on contemporary capitalism," you signal the "becoming-rent of profit": the classical Weberian entrepreneur is no longer a plausible figurehead for economic activity and growth, as he has been replaced by speculators on financial markets. That being the case, what can we expect in the (near) future, in terms of further repetitions of debt-driven crises?

AF: In bio-cognitive capitalism, the becoming-rent of profit means that an increasing share of surplus value derives from forms of primitive accumulation in terms of extractive activity and dispossession. Some human activities (especially the cognitive-relational ones) are able to self-organize, even in a partial way. Entrepreneurial activity today is characterized by a coordination activity thanks to the reinforcement of private property (especially intellectual property and private financial concentration), to allow for the extraction of surplus value. This situation leads to increasing instability and new forms of indirect command and power (neoliberal governance). That means that crisis will be a normal state in capitalist accumulation, instead of being exceptional.

9. Interview with Costas Lapavitsas

Arjen Kleinherenbrink

Costas Lapavitsas is a Greek politician and professor of economics at the School of Oriental and African Studies at the University of London. His research concerns critical examinations of the globalized financial system, particularly in the context of the Greek government-debt crisis, the Eurozone crisis and the euro currency. His recent works include *Word for Word: Writings on the Greek Crisis* (in Greek, 2014) and *Profiting Without Producing: How Finance Exploits Us All* (2013).

Arjen Kleinherenbrink: Our conversation roughly coincides with the tenth "anniversary" of the 2007-2008 financial crisis. In a 2014 piece for The Guardian *("Finance's hold on our everyday life must be broken"), you concluded that 6 years after the crisis, very little had changed and that financialization was apparently here to stay. Where are we now, for example if we look at financial products being traded, the dynamic of financial markets, and governmental policies? Now that 4 more years have passed, do you see any developments that might warrant a more optimistic view? Or are we simply heading for the next crisis?*

Costas Lapavitsas: Let me say, first of all, that I understand financialization as a historical period. I think that the clearest meaning of the term is that it is a period of change in the development of mature capitalism. I have to stress this because, as the literature on financialization keeps expanding, the term is becoming less and less clear. People use it in all kinds of contexts and often without any precision, which creates confusion. I use the term in a specific sense: to indicate a historical period of change that has lasted roughly 4 decades now.

We are still in a period of financialized capitalism. Mature countries remain financialized – with differences among them – and developing countries are displaying strong tendencies toward financialization. However, if we look at the 10 years since the outbreak of the crisis, particularly at the United States – where the core of financialization lies – financialization is at a watershed. It has not advanced with anything like the speed and dynamism of the previous 20 years. In a sense, financialization has stopped in the United States, something that can be witnessed in two key areas. First, financial profits have not been increasing in a sustained way. Rather, they have been stagnant, or even falling, for much of the previous decade. Second and crucially, household debt has been declining as a proportion of gross domestic product for the first time since the post-war period. These are marks of stagnant financialization, and it is not clear how things will develop in this respect in the USA in the coming years.

Much will depend on which policies the US government will choose to adopt. I do not think that another bout of explosive financialization is very likely, but of course it always remains possible. However, the more likely scenario is that this "flat" performance of financialization will continue, which implies a stagnating real economy, with an ever-present possibility of financial crisis. For the fact that financialization is not expanding does not mean that we are now done with crises. Perhaps we will not have another gigantic crisis similar to 2007-2009, but we might very well have another significant financial crisis in the near future. After all, the processes of financial excess have not stopped, even if financialization is not expanding dynamically. Currently, the US stock market is already showing all the signs of a bubble, and that could lead to a financial crisis in the near future.

AK: What do you think are the causes of this "watershed" at which financialization has arrived?

CL: If we look at the USA, there are three key elements. First, the productive sector of the economy (i.e. non-financial enterprises) has not increased its debt significantly. There is little or no increase in the reliance of non-financial enterprises on credit from banks and other financial institutions. Non-financial profits have risen (because they are squeezing their workers very hard), but at the same time investment remains weak. This is also true for Europe and a number of other countries. Second, US households, which were one of the driving forces of the accumulation of debt in the previous period, have been reducing their exposure. Household debt has two components: mortgages and consumer debt. Consumer debt has recovered after the crisis, but it is not increasing all that fast. And since mortgages constitute a much larger portion of household debt, consumer debt alone could not determine the evolution of total household borrowing. The key development in this respect is that mortgage debt has been declining. Third, financial debt (debt between banks or between banks and other institutions, the type that can generate profits through churning of loanable capital or through transacting with each other) has shrunk substantially.

The only significant *increase* in debt concerns state debt. As a counterpart to quantitative easing, the US government has been borrowing heavily. The state has been providing the financial system with abundant liquidity to allow it to survive the crisis, but in order to do so, it had to accumulate huge debts. In sum, we have had a decline in private debt, but an increase in public debt. Financialization has been stagnant, but it has been supported by the state which has heavily indebted itself. The crisis has ushered in a period in which financialization has come to depend on the state much more than before.

AK: If we shift our attention from the US to Europe, one could (perhaps somewhat cynically) argue that the EU response to the Greek government-debt crisis in the wake of the financial crisis has served as a "test case" for both proponents and critics of the monetary union's status quo – specifically when it comes to how peripheral European countries remain economically shackled to the EU core via debt, to the effects of such a situation, and to responding to such effects. What do you think are the key lessons both sides (take themselves to) have learned?

CL: There are many lessons here, the question is where to start. If we look at Greece, what we have is a historic disaster. In a sense, it is the classic disaster of a country with a relatively weak economy adopting a hard currency, thinking that the hard currency would help it create a stronger economy. That is the *oldest* fallacy in monetary economics. When you adopt a hard currency with an economy that is not up to it, you simply destroy that economy. This is evident in the case of Greece, which has accepted repeated bail-out agreements to remain in the monetary union, the last one having been signed by the Syriza government in August 2015. Several months later, in May 2016, the Syriza government also accepted a framework for the Greek national debt, which, together with the bail-out terms, has set the country's course for the near future. Concretely, this will mean severe austerity measures in government finances, that is, restraining public expenditure and imposing high taxes, but without any significant debt reduction. There will also be continued liberalization and privatization in the labor market and other areas of the economy, in the hope that neoliberal reform will lead to growth. This is the package that the Greek ruling elite has accepted in order to stay in the euro.

The outcome of this incredibly tough set of arrangements was predictable. The Greek economy has shrunk enormously since 2008 and the prospects for growth remain weak. Policies such as these are further destroying any possibility of sustained growth.

The notion that applying austerity while at the same time liberalizing markets is capable of generating growth as private enterprises increase their investment reflects the worst kind of neoliberal economics. Capitalist development simply does not happen that way. Greece is looking at long-term weakness, with a stabilized, but struggling economy. Young people will emigrate and the country will become increasingly marginal in Europe.

This casts light on two important developments regarding the EMU. First, the euro is a very rigid and unbending mechanism of austerity and liberalization. Moreover, if we look at the decision-making processes in the EMU, decisions are typically made in Berlin, not in Brussels. Germany plays the decisive role in the European Union. That is not academic speculation but a plain fact of life in Europe. Using Greece as a convenient lever, Germany has asserted its dominance in the European Union during the last 10 years. The euro has emerged as a site of strongly hierarchical mechanisms to implement austerity and liberalization policies, which are emanating from Berlin. Second, ideologically, the euro has proven itself as an incredibly efficient mechanism to discipline labor, but also more broadly the people of Europe. This is a somewhat new phenomenon that we are witnessing in Europe. We have always known that money is a very powerful ideological instrument, but the power of the euro over the people of Europe is simply astonishing. It is an incredible disciplinary device, as we have seen in Greece and elsewhere. A key element of the last French election that made for Macron's victory, for example, was the mobilization of *fear* of exiting the monetary union. Thus, even the French population has been disciplined and scared by the euro. Any broad economic struggle in the future will have to take the disciplining power of the euro into account.

AK: It also seems as if one cannot be skeptical about the euro without immediately being associated with the (Far) Right. We seem to believe that a critical attitude towards the euro coincides with xenophobia and nationalistic fantasies...

CL: This is a very unfortunate, indeed a disastrous, political development, and it must be traced to the broader attitude of the Left. After the collapse of the Soviet Bloc and the signing of the Maastricht Treaty, the European Left effectively stopped believing in radical, structural change in Europe. It tacitly accepted that some kind of capitalism is inevitable. It started to believe that the EU and the EMU were inherently benign institutions that allowed for a better management of capitalism. This view has become deeply entrenched in the ideological DNA of much of the European Left. The conclusion drawn by many is that left-wing political forces must struggle to make these institutions even "friendlier" for working people. This is an argument that significant parts of the Right have never accepted.

As the euro backfired after 2010, much of the Left found itself in an impossible position. To argue something *relevant*, it had to challenge the very existence of the European institutions and especially the monetary union. But it could not bring itself to do so because it had accepted the benign nature of European institutions and no longer believed that *structurally different* social arrangements were possible in Europe. As a result, the Left found itself unable to propose radical policies that could make sense to large numbers of working people in Europe, whose conditions steadily deteriorated as a result of policies to defend the euro. In contrast, the Right actively exploited the opportunity of the crisis and, of course, channeled the frustration and anger of the people in the wrong direction. After all, the working class in most European countries has never been in favor of the European Union or of the monetary union. These were never projects that operated from "the bottom up." Since the Left has stopped responding to working people's worries and problems with radical proposals, it is not surprising that they have turned to the Right.

AK: You mentioned the 2016 framework that will set Greece on a path of continued austerity politics. Yet, at the same time, we're also increasingly hearing that the IMF is now backpedaling its earlier infatuation with austerity measures. Should such signals be taken seriously? What are the chances that policy makers will respond to future crises with measures that are different from repeated austerity politics?

CL: Germany and France brought the IMF to Europe in the context of the Eurozone crisis. European elites realized that they would have to take some very tough measures, and they needed a vehicle to legitimize them. In truth, the main proponent of austerity in Europe has always been the EU bureaucracy, and much less the IMF. The IMF has never been the real "bad guy." We've seen this with the IMF before: a domestic ruling class wants to impose strict economic measures, but knowing that these will be deeply unpopular, it conveniently blames the IMF. The hardest proponents of austerity and neoliberal reform were found within the EU itself.

In Greece, for instance, the IMF was keen to streamline the state sector with a view to increasing the tax income and reducing expenditure. The European Commission, however, wanted to intervene and reshape the very *structure* of the Greek economy and society. This attitude, which has been fully documented, was troubling for the IMF. Moreover, the IMF stated from the very beginning of the crisis that Greece needed debt relief, and it also said that policies such as those applied in Greece would typically require an exchange rate devaluation. That is what the IMF would have typically demanded for any country outside the Eurozone. But, of course, devaluation was impossible within the monetary union, and the European Central Bank was adamant that there would be no debt relief. It is quite clear that the EU has always been the most rigid component of the troika.

This indicates that policies followed by Europe have resulted from choices made by the most powerful and least flexible components of European capitalism. It spells deep trouble for the future of Europe – and the IMF realizes this. However, the IMF is not powerful enough to change things. The problem, in other words, is Europe itself, its structures and class differences, not the IMF.

AK: Could you elaborate on what you here mean by class differences?

CL: Europe today is only tenuously related to Europe before the crisis. It is a very different beast. I have already mentioned the dominant position of the German elites in EU decision-making. Where does this dominance come from? Obviously from Germany's economic power, particularly from its export surplus and its concomitant ability to lend. Why is German capitalism so economically powerful? It is certainly *not* because of its investment, technological progress or dynamic growth. I stress this because people tend to get very confused about Germany. They think it is some kind of miracle country, a place where capitalism is surging ahead and creating new frontiers. Nothing could be further from the truth! Germany is a place of weak domestic investment and weak productivity growth. It is a country that lives with persistent austerity. This is clearly seen in public provision and in poor infrastructure. Germany's domestic economy is not dynamic.

However, *externally*, Germany is incredibly successful, with a tremendous surplus in relation to markets within and outside Europe. This surplus comes from its industrial sector, the core strength of German capitalism (mostly automobiles, chemicals and machine goods). But where does this tremendous strength of industrial exports come from? In a nutshell, it is primarily based on wage suppression and on a precarious labor market that generates poor conditions for the majority of German workers. The suppression of wages is the result of reforms that were brought in by the Schröder government in the late nineties. *That* is the secret of German success: wage suppression that gives German capital a competitive advantage despite a relative lack of investment and productivity growth. German surpluses have been achieved *at the expense* of German workers, and big business has been reaping the profits. Germany has become far more inequitable, with the gap between the poor and rich increasing due to the various pressures on labor. What we see is a country dominated by a privileged industrial elite in cahoots with big banks.

In addition, we have also seen the emergence of a new periphery in Europe. It is not the peripheral South (Greece, Portugal, Spain) that we already know. The German industrial core has created a second periphery for itself, consisting of Poland, Hungary, the Czech Republic, Slovakia and Slovenia. These countries are now attached to the German industrial complex. German foreign direct investment has spread to them, transforming their economies in its own image. Moreover, the German industrial core has also pulled toward itself the economies of other EU core countries, like Austria and the Netherlands.

This is the present reality of Europe, the true source of power and the driving force of EU development. Austerity and neoliberal reform fit the interests of German industrial capital and banks, as does a Europe that is split into a Germany-dominated core and dependent peripheries. This is the reality behind the increasing differences between rich and poor in the EU, the harsh, aggressive and exploitative capitalism that we are now witnessing. The ideology of the European Union is a very convenient façade for it.

AK: To follow up on your remarks concerning the increasing precarization of labor and the widening difference between rich and poor: the question here is of course why people are not protesting…In your book Crisis in the Eurozone, *you also describe how the burden of the financial crisis has been passed onto working people in the form of reduced wages and pensions, higher unemployment, unraveling of the welfare state and so on. Yet in a 2014 piece in* The Guardian, *you also note the surprising lack of protest against this, especially among young people. Whence this lack? Or put differently: how can it be that young people* do *seem prepared to protest "cultural" problems (identity politics and so on), but not economic ones?*

CL: That's an important question. One thing I have learned by being involved in Greek politics is that it is very difficult to predict popular responses. One can assess the political economy of the direction of capitalism with reasonable accuracy, but assessing popular responses is extremely hard. Nevertheless, two things seem important here. First, we *have* seen strong reactions, but as you rightly say, they often take the form of identity politics (concerning gender, sexual preferences, racial issues, religious beliefs and so on) and the defense of democratic rights. Second, we have seen reactions that are associated with the Right, which is *also* mobilizing identity politics in order to promote its own agenda – often with an authoritarian or fascist content. The question then becomes, why have we not witnessed sustained protests with truly progressive demands, politically and economically?

A very important element in this is again the underlying weakness of the Left. There was a time when the Left would have proposed to the European people a clear program of radical, democratic economic and social change, and it would have done so with the aim of challenging capitalism itself. It would have proposed a vision of a different kind of society – not simply an anti-capitalist vision, but an alternative *socialist* vision. The European Left always had a strong component that was audacious enough to say that it is possible to build a non-capitalist society, a socialist society, to give it its proper name. Unfortunately, that has been largely lost. But if the Left does not argue for a socialist society, it will always find itself in a weak position. You can defend democracy and argue for minority rights and so on all you like, but in the end, you will not be offering a decisive breakthrough that would have real popular resonance.

We have also come to realize that a key issue in this respect is sovereignty. The way that working people experience economic pressures in their everyday lives, but also the various kinds of pressures associated with identity (think of migration, for example), is as a loss of sovereignty. Academics often imagine that ordinary people do not understand the complexity of sovereignty, but they understand it very well indeed. For ordinary people, the last 10 years have been 10 years of loss of sovereignty in the simple but powerful sense of: "I do not control my environment at all. I am simply moved about by other people's decisions, and there is nothing I can do about it." This everyday experience gets replicated at a higher level, where people feel that their own countries are now unable to defend the basic rights and provisions that are at the heart of distinct cultural groups and nations.

The Left has been most reluctant to tackle the issue of sovereignty and to devise a post-capitalist program that warrants popular as well as national sovereignty. It has lost its bearings on this point, because it thinks that this is somehow a reactionary issue that could only lead to the resurgence of nationalism. This is wrong. Popular sovereignty is by no means a negation of internationalism, and left-wing internationalism is not the same thing as big-business internationalism. If the Left cannot offer people some form of sovereignty, then the Right will do it in its own poisonous way – which is exactly what is happening now.

AK: There is no real alternative for people to rally behind...

CL: What is needed is to connect economic issues and social injustices, such as the widening gap between rich and poor, to the question of sovereignty in the political and national domain. We need a powerful political combination of these elements – which is precisely what the Left used to provide. It used to propose programs intending to overturn the capitalist system and at the same time empower people in their everyday lives. Unfortunately, it no longer does it, and that is a point of decisive importance.

AK: This makes me think of your proposal for a return to national, sovereign currencies in the EU. Do you argue for the abandonment of the euro in favor of national currencies, or for national currencies that would exist alongside the euro? And is such a return still a plausible option?

CL: Let's be clear about one thing. In terms of what it *promised* to do when it was introduced, the euro and the European monetary union have failed completely. The euro was supposed to be a mechanism for convergence, shared prosperity, increased economic balance among the nations of Europe, collegiality, all these wonderful things. It promised to be the glue that would hold us all together. It has done the exact opposite. It has functioned as a mechanism for fostering hierarchies between core and periphery, it has exacerbated national tensions, it has alienated people from their immediate economic and institutional frameworks, and it has made the totality of the EU much more unstable. In these respects, the euro has failed. Nonetheless, it has been defended and even made harder by the German industrial machine and the ruling classes of Europe.

For me, it is simply a matter of time before the euro comes to an end. It is a deeply diseased mechanism, one that has only become worse over the past 10 years. But, because of how the EU has developed institutionally, dismantling the euro is now far more difficult than it would have been 10 years ago. For a country like Greece (and a number of other peripheral countries), exiting is now a matter of historical survival. As long as Greece remains in the euro, its decline is guaranteed. We know from considerable research that an exit is feasible. It is a difficult process that would take some bravery and some strong decision-making by domestic forces. It would also require that working people take a lead – but it can be done.

For core countries like France, Germany and the Netherlands, the situation is not the same as for Greece. There, the Left must propose a new way of organizing trade and economic interaction among the countries of Europe. This is because we do not want to go back to a system of competing national economies. Recovering national sovereignty does not mean going back to competing, warring nations – it is simply a myth that this would have to be the case. Control over how and where people live is part of internationalism. The Left in core countries must go beyond the re-imposition of national currencies and propose mechanisms that allow for balanced and amicable arrangements of transactions between European nations, on the basis of solidarity. We know that this can be done – both technically and politically. It is just a matter of political and social choice. If the Left begins to propose it, it will acquire political relevance.

AK: This reminds me of how Marx distinguishes between internationalism and globalization / cosmopolitanism.

CL: That's exactly right. The Left cannot be for globalization and cosmopolitanism, which is what big business wants. We are not for the freedom of capital to move between countries; we are not for the unfettered freedom to sell commodities anywhere one pleases; and we are not for the freedom of capital to shift individual workers from country to country without any protection, without housing, without fitting into the framework of the country in which you live. All that is not internationalism as the Left understands it but internationalism as capital understands it. As far as I am concerned, the Left that I belong to is against that.

AK: Unfortunately, that Left is not very strong at the moment...

CL: I know, but we have to keep arguing for it!

AK: In Profiting without Producing, *you propose a shift to public ownership of and control over banks. What would the advantages of this shift be, and how would it be different from a nationalization of banks?*

CL: This proposal should be understood in the context of definancialization. We began talking about financialization, so we might as well close our discussion with that. If one wants to challenge capitalism today, one has to pay attention to definancialization (and potentially deglobalization). Definancialization has many aspects, and one of the elements that it must contain is the radical transformation of the financial system, in the direction of introducing public ownership and control. The European (and international) financial system has grown tremendously, but it certainly does not operate in a recognizably capitalist way according to the textbooks. We have a system that makes tremendous profits, but depends on the state to protect it, to provide it with liquidity, to incur large debts on behalf of it, and to support it in times of crisis. What kind of capitalism is that?

We need new banks and new financial institutions to support investment, public spending and private consumption, and to enable people to make choices that actually suit their lives.

Public banks are necessary and, of course, several already exist, but they have to be transformed. We need public banks that would operate with a strong spirit of public service. That does not mean that they would provide free money. There would be accountability and clear reference terms for the operations of public banks providing funds for long-term investment and consumption but also for the safekeeping and the transfer of money. If we intervened in the financial system in this way, we would remove some of the power of private banks, forcing them to begin to behave in a different way. This could further be strengthened through controls over transactions among financial institutions and controls over the movement of capital between countries. It is a very ambitious proposal, but it can be done. Those who deny it typically speak for the interests of private finance.

Another important aspect of definancialization has to do with households. Private finance has penetrated deeply into the realm of households. People borrow for housing, health, education, consumption and so on. Finance mediates an incredible range of decisions taken by working people and it is far from the most appropriate mediation. To definancialize society it is important to deal with housing, schooling, health and other issues in ways that fundamentally rely on public provision, not on private provision mediated by finance. This will reduce the power of finance and directly challenge contemporary capitalism, allowing socialist ideas to gain more traction in the lives of ordinary people.

AK: One final question. It might be the case that no change is possible as long as the central paradigmatic idea (or fantasy) of contemporary capitalism is not challenged: the idea that perpetual growth is the cure-all for everything, so that – obviously – nothing can be allowed to stand in the way of more growth. So, if one proposes to reinvigorate public provisions and welfare institutions, the immediate objection will be that this limits opportunities for growth...

CL: Well, let's recall a few simple facts. The fastest period of growth in post-war capitalism occurred in the 1950s and 1960s, decades in which we *had* some public provision and some control over capital. In contrast, the last 4 decades of neoliberalism and freedom for private capital have been very bad for growth. Needless to say, I am not arguing for a return to the 1950s and 1960s, but we must start by acknowledging historical reality. The policies of deregulation, privatization, cutting public provisions and so on have been very bad for growth.

Growth is necessary. But we need growth that is socially decided upon, growth that has social conditions and requirements. It needs to be determined in a democratic and collective manner, and it must take into account the environment as well as the evolution of social needs. That is the kind of growth we need, rather than a blind fixation on growth for its own sake.

10. Interview with Maurizio Lazzarato

Erik Bordeleau and Sjoerd van Tuinen[1]

Translated from French by Erik Bordeleau and revised by Joel E. Mason

Maurizio Lazzarato is an Italian sociologist and philosopher based in Paris. As an activist during the 1970s in the Autonomia Operaia (Italian labor movement), he was forced into exile to escape legal proceedings. His most recent work deals with the question of debt, war and semio-capitalism: *The Making of the Indebted Man* (Semiotext(e), 2012); *Signs and Machines: Capitalism and the Production of Subjectivity* (MIT Press, 2014); *Governing by Debt* (Semiotext(e), 2015); and more recently, with Eric Alliez, *Guerre et Capital* (Amsterdam, 2016).

Erik Bordeleau: After the financial crisis of 2007, you yourself, together with David Graeber, were among the first to search for the moral, anthropological and theological roots of debt as the ancestral condition of capitalism. We witness a monetary turn in political philosophy that mobilizes radically heterodox genealogies. Where do you situate yourself within this monetary turn? When did you start identifying debt as a key problem? And how would you describe your own method of analysis?

Maurizio Lazzarato: Financial capitalism has a completely different relationship to money than industrial capitalism. Marxism has mostly focused on industrial capitalism; its critique of financial capitalism is not as developed (the third book of Marx's *Capital* is little more than a series of notes). It is therefore difficult to grasp the relationship that financial capitalism maintains with money.

The genealogy that underlies my research is twofold: it is both French and Italian. There is a fundamental moment to understanding financial capitalism: on August 15, 1971, Nixon declared the dollar unconvertible to gold, thus ending the Bretton Woods agreement. Currency becomes a self-referential tautology – one dollar equals one dollar. It no longer has any relation with an economic substrate. Money is transformed into a directly political element.

In 1971-1972, two important texts were produced. First in 1971, even before Nixon's declaration, there is a course by Michel Foucault on ancient Greece, where he discusses the institution of money (in fact, it is the only place in his work where he deals directly with this problem). It tells how Cypselos introduced the use of currency in Corinth in the seventh century BC. Foucault shows how the invention of money meets two problems: the problem of debt and the problem of war. Cypselos formed an army with poor peasants to drive away the aristocracy. Once he had won, the armed peasant force became a political force. To territorialize this deterritorialization of the political force assumed by the indebted peasants, Cypselos invented an economic circuit that is organized around money. The fundamental element to note here is that money is not born from economic exchange, or from labor as in Marx, but from debt and war.

The other fundamental text of the genealogy of currency that I propose is, obviously, Deleuze and Guattari's *Anti-Oedipus*, which dates from 1972. If we set aside the critique of psychoanalysis, *Anti-Oedipus* appears as a great work on the question of money. Deleuze and Guattari make it clear: money is debt. They produce a new theory of money at just about the same time that we enter a new monetary regime that is no longer based on convertibility with gold. For some time now, I have been following the question of debt in Deleuze's work, which he develops in Nietzsche's wake and which offers an exploration path outside of the Marxist framework. And there is this sentence that finally convinced me to write on the subject, which appears in his famous "Postscript on the Societies of Control": "A man is no longer a man confined, but a man in debt."

And then, on the Italian side, there was a whole series of discussions in the magazine *Primo Maggio* on the monetary question in 1973-74, but it did not go as far as what Deleuze and Guattari proposed. These two have clearly established that the territorializing force of currency is directly linked to the deterritorializing force of war.

EB: In The Making of the Indebted Man, *you argue that the economy of debt fully realizes the mode of governmental management of the political, the social, the economic, the state, etc., described by Foucault in the late 1970s – even though governing by debt is no longer liberal but increasingly authoritarian. Then in* Governing by Debt, *you become more critical of Foucault. You argue that instead of liberal governmentality, we have never been dealing with anything other than state capitalism, and an ongoing battle over the welfare state. What exactly is your critique of liberal governmentality and thus also of Foucault's liberalism, and what role does debt play in this context?*

ML: It is a rather polemical argument. In his course on neoliberalism, Foucault is perhaps the first to carry out, almost in real time, an analysis of how capitalism is taking a new shape. But strangely, there is no reference to the problem of money. I argue that fundamentally, the weapon of neoliberalism is the triad of money-credit-debt, through which new forms of governmentality are established. This absence can probably be explained by the abandonment of Foucault's criticism of political economy, a path that Deleuze and Guattari did not follow. The latter remained close to the Marxist definition of capitalism, but in a very clever way; they did so less through the notion of work than through that of money.

Foucault, at that time at least, took another route. He read liberalism as an innovation in the field of governmentality. It is an interesting way to pose the problem, but it leaves aside the question of war. The transition from Fordism to post-Fordism must be conceived not as a purely economic or monetary transition, but as a strategic operation. By strategy, I mean a war relation, where there are adversaries, a struggle. And capitalism does have a strategy, it is to dismantle the constraint that they had to integrate into the system because of the Russian Revolution. This point of view is completely lacking in Foucault's analysis, although we cannot deny the great relevance of his analysis of the new forms of subjectivity, the entrepreneur of the self, and so on. And this omission is all the more astonishing because he had brilliantly thematized the question of the relationship between war and politics in previous years.

So, I think we have to keep the problem of governmentality, but we need to conceive of it as a war continued by other means. Even the transition from Fordism to neoliberalism is based on a civil war, although it did not deploy all the violence of the civil wars of the first half of the twentieth century. I'm thinking here of May '68 and its repercussions. Obviously, May '68 did not really endanger capitalism in the manner of the Russian Revolution or the political movements of the late nineteenth century.

That said, it is important to remember that, despite the strategic weakness of the '68 movement, a civil war was raging in Latin America, coinciding with the shift toward a new mode of production. They bombed President Allende in Chile, massacred the Argentine people...What happened in Italy is nothing compared to what happened in Latin America. It is a civil war that they won in a military-political way. It was only later that the Chicago boys disembarked and, allied with the fascists, led the first neoliberal experiments. Foucault did not consider that. This is the danger of looking only at the innovative character of neoliberalism.

Foucault of course does not stop there. In his 1982 article, "The Subject and Power," he makes an important distinction, often ignored by his commentators, between strategic relationships and power relations. He says that relations of power are relations between rulers and governed; strategic relationships are the relations between adversaries. The problem is thus to pass from the relationship between opponents to a relationship of governmentality and vice versa. So, if we go back to post-Fordism from this perspective, we see that at some point the strategic confrontation has been won by Capital, and it is based on this victory that new relations of power are elaborated – the neoliberal devices – to determine more or less predictably the conduct of others.

EB: In your last book with E. Alliez, War and Capital, *you focus on the intimate relationship between capital and war. You present an idea of total war that goes beyond class struggle and involves race, gender and, first of all, subjectivity. How do you define the concept of civil war? And how do you relate to other contemporary thinkers who also take up the Foucauldian (and Schmittian) analyses of the concept of civil war (I think of Bernard Aspe or the Invisible Committee, for example)?*

ML: For me, the problem is very simple: we have to deal with the question of war in a precise and targeted way, in close connection with a conceptualization of capitalism, which is not the case with the Invisible Committee. This is what we sought to establish in our book. Schmitt, or Clausewitz for that matter, make very serious analyses of war, but without relating it to capitalism. For example: when war encounters the infinite valorization of capitalism, it begets total war. In *War and Capital*, we have tried to identify the decisive moments in which capitalism, states and war are transforming themselves. In this respect, the analysis of the Invisible Committee seems insufficient...

EB:...because they do not introduce a theory of the regimes of a-signifying signs such as the one you elaborate in the wake of Guattari's work?

ML: The clearest example of an a-signifying regime of signs is precisely money. Money is an a-signifying sign, that is, its function does not pass through consciousness; it operates mechanically or molecularly, as Guattari puts it. For instance, we're cutting interest rates by half a point, and there's a series of immediate repercussions in people's lives. The difficulty here, and it is the same with regard to technology and its power of automation exemplified in algorithmic governmentality, concerns the fact that this machinic operation doesn't happen without producing remnants. There is always a strategic dimension that technological automatism cannot contain. The machine has socio-political organs that subjectivize it. The problem, then, is to think together of an a-signifying and mechanistic regime, largely automatic, while at the same time leaving a place for strategic relations. The social machine does not coincide with the technical machine, for the social machine is always also a machine of war, that is, animated by strategic relations between adversaries. It is important to emphasize this. Let us take the example of 1971: the monetary machine had begun to jam. The declaration of inconvertibility that followed was not an "automatism": it was a strategic choice that gave rise to the emergence of new automatisms, new devices of power. Discontinuities within capitalism presuppose not only economic, technological and monetary "revolutions," but also political-military victories.

EB: This strategic light, when cast on the decisions that underpin contemporary finance, reframes – and re-politicizes – the problem of debt...

ML: Debt is another way to wage war. I think of those two generals of the Chinese air force who wrote this book, *Unrestricted Warfare*. They say nothing else. They describe the policies of the International Monetary Fund in Southeast Asia as a non-bloody war waged with financial rather than military means. I think they are right. How to say it? Financial capitalism is not an anomaly of capital. It is a profound tendency carried from the very beginning: C – M – C' becomes essentially: C – C'. It is its true nature coming into expression. This was already the case in the hegemonic capitalism of the late nineteenth century. Beginning in 1870, we already have the premises of financial capitalism. Colonialism is financial capitalism. France and England at the time are countries living off colonial rents. And this financial capitalism caused the First World War, the Second also; it also led to the Russian Revolution etc. Fifty years of war and more than a hundred million deaths. It's a lot. In the post-war period, capitalism was obliged to deal with the labor movement. But as soon as the workers' movement came into crisis after 1968, financial capitalism recovered and reformulated itself. It is a new financial capitalism in which debt plays a fundamental role, because everything is being reorganized around the creditor-debtor relationship. You have to see it as a strategic operation, the continuation of war by other means.

It is on this basis that we must integrate the conceptual developments of Nietzsche, and of Deleuze after him, into the forms of culpability related to debt. The economic or monetary turn requires new forms of subjectivity.

EB: *I would be very curious to hear you say more about the different alternatives that might arise in response to this undisputed dominance by the means of financialization. I am thinking of the growing interest in community and complementary currencies; the revival of jubilee practices and other collective debt payments (student or others); and also the promises that some see in the emergence of crypto-currencies or blockchain as a tool to redistribute the value captured by online platforms. I am thinking, for example, of the Economic Space Agency founded by Akseli Virtanen, which I recently took part in, a follow-up to the Robin Hood Hedge Fund Coop project. How do you envisage the emergence of new financial war machines?*

ML: What is meant by a war machine? What relationships are forged between the war machine and the technical machine? The simplest example that comes to mind is what happened with Nuit debout in France in 2016 during the movement against the Labor Act. Nuit debout occupied Place de la République and in 2 days they managed to master communication methods like television and radio. That is to say, they integrated them into their war machine. At the same time, they have failed to develop a real strategy for their war machine. I'll give two examples. First, they have failed to break the separation between the white precarious young people of central Paris and the immigrants who reside in the suburbs. And they have not been able to dissolve the division between precarious and standard employees. So, for me, the challenge for the creation of war machines is not technological; it is rather social and political. Virtual networking basically relies on effective social networks. If you do not rely on strong and transversal social networks, your information does not cross the physical border of the device, nor does it reach standard employees.

Let us therefore say that I am *a priori* quite skeptical of the so-called technological solutions to the existing politico-financial problems. There are a lot of experiments going on right now. From a theoretical point of view, for me, the question of debt is essentially linked to that of war; and in this sense money is used to territorialize war. One must bear in mind the power structures that are built to governmentalize this territorialization. I am concerned that the experiments lack strategic perspective on the current war. We are very attached to forms of collective collaboration and mobilization. But capital is not merely a production to be diverted to collaborative forms, as some post-operative comrades tend to believe. It is a matter of war. The crisis of 2008 has shown it clearly: the capitalist machine, which can give the impression of being on autopilot, needs the social organs of control, management and intervention because it only functions when things go wrong, that is to say: it proceeds by crises. It is not the algorithms that have produced austerity plans. And we cannot simply oppose forms of cooperation to strategic forms. As soon as the mechanisms underlying the debt system begin to jam, the horizon of war is immediately visible.

EB: Could you then tell us more about the relationship between debt and liquidity production? Following the work of Keynes, Amato and Fantacci in their book Ends of Finance, *for example, locate the problem of contemporary finance in its obsession with liquidity. What do you think of this kind of post-Keynesian problematization?*

ML: I think we must conceive of liquidity as a higher level of abstraction, to speak in Marxist terms. To make money more liquid, and to make exchanges more liquid, it is this higher level of abstraction of social relations which is the object of control and domination. Clearly, we have not been able to raise ourselves to the level of abstraction at which debt policy is established.

EB: We are thus brought back to the famous question formulated by Mackenzie Wark during Occupy Wall Street: How to occupy an abstraction?

ML: Indeed, it is difficult to rise to the degree of deterritorialization imposed by financial capitalism essentially because within the Marxist tradition, as I stressed at the beginning, one is accustomed to reflect with theoretical tools forged in response to industrial capitalism. There is a bankruptcy at the strategic level. About liquidity: I do not think we can control it in a Keynesian fashion anymore. Regulation was also a political fact. There were forces which made this regulation possible and necessary: the crisis of 1929 on the one hand, and the Russian Revolution on the other. Braudel wrote: in 1914, Europe was ready to tip into socialism. It was war that prevented this tilting, transforming the internationalist worker into a nationalist soldier. And immediately after the war, we see the explosion of the Russian Revolution; revolutionary movements in Germany, Italy etc. It is this threat of regime overthrow that has led to regulation. It is not regulated for economic reasons, but for strategic reasons.

EB: This is the common objection made to Piketty...

ML: The problem of liquidity, "the euthanasia of the rentiers" as Keynes has it, is not settled from within capital, as if it were wiser for it to proceed in this way. Capital aims at infinite valorization. And the only way to block this infinite valorization logic is to cause it problems. With the Russian Revolution, capitalists feared for their lives, and it was only because of this that they conceded certain compromises.

EB: That reminds me of a meeting in Stuttgart in 2014 between you, Peter Pál Pelbart, Akseli Virtanen and Brian Massumi. Towards the end of that conversation, you emphasize the decisive importance of the Leninist moment. This contrasts with the manner in which Massumi, for example, seeks to think of ontogenetic counterpowers "at the end of the economy," without a revolutionary historical reference.

ML: It is a question that also arises with some post-operative comrades. I think we are engaged in an incredible series of defeats. Let us take the case of France: there has been an exceptional popular mobilization against the Labor Act which did not prevent this law from being voted into existence a year later. As soon as he won the elections, Macron hastened to further reduce the already weakened rights of workers. It was as if the struggle had not existed. Obviously, something is wrong. We don't seem to be able to threaten the machine. I do not like to think that there are always possibilities and opportunities. Historically, I think the current class composition is weaker than that of the late nineteenth century because it does not pose the political problem in terms of revolution. It does not seek to end capitalism as such. They were able to occupy Paris, capital of the nineteenth century, for 2 months...it is as if we occupied New York today! Well, they were massacred, but Lenin then built his speech on the defeat of the Commune. So, if we do not accept that we were beaten, that 1968 was a defeat, we will not achieve anything. Without an effective war machine, the possibilities maintained by a certain left remain in vain. But for now, I do not see the beginning of a beginning to this story.

EB: On the basis of this observation, it may be necessary to open up an ethical-aesthetic dimension, the one that you sometimes entertain in your writings when you talk about demobilization or when you take up Deleuze and Guattari's concept of "anti-production." How does one evade the empire of valorization in 2017? Or from another angle perhaps: what is the actuality of Italian autonomia's politics?

ML: I understand the fascination of the people of your generation for Italian autonomy, but hey, we must still remember that we were defeated. If I now live in France, it is because I was exiled. Lenin elaborated a hypothesis that led to a first victorious revolution, with all its imperfections, because he did not simply make a hymn to the Paris Commune and its 30,000 executed people.

EB: Let me then reformulate: how does one escape from the subjective form of the entrepreneur of oneself?

ML: Yes, it is with this kind of problem in view that I published this little book about Marcel Duchamp and the refusal of work. It takes a moment of rupture, of subjective affirmation. Without it, it becomes very difficult to develop a space of political resistance. Therefore: the refusal of work as an interruption of the normal functioning of the capitalist machine. And from there it becomes possible to think of the development of war machines. Labor is the institution of capital. We cannot be saved by labor, because labor is not an anthropological constant that goes through the ages and which capitalism appropriated. Labor was invented by capitalism. Or to say it with Deleuze and Guattari: overwork precedes work. In this sense, the capitalist form precedes labor. My little book on Duchamp is an attempt to mark the rejection and to distinguish it from the celebration of forms of cooperation, or rather: forms of cooperation are fine, but only in so far as they are clearly based on a refusal and a rupture.

EB: *In conclusion: Angela Merkel has included in her program a promise of full employment within 8 years. What does this takeover of an old demand of the Left mean under the neoliberal condition of the indebted man? And what future do you see for Europe in political and financial terms?*

ML: The only full employment possible now is full precarious employment. And in this context, and since the crisis of 2008, what we see in Europe is the rise of discourse on war, the rise of new forms of fascism (not to speak of the new President of the United States). That's what I think is essential. There are new political forces that occupy public space by declaring war on immigrants, refugees and so on. We must take these forms of "sly" civil war very seriously.

11. Interview with Tomáš Sedláček

Arjen Kleinherenbrink

Tomáš Sedláček is a Czech economist, university lecturer and macroeconomic strategist. He is a former member of the National Economic Council of the Czech Republic and an economic adviser to former president Václav Havel. His *Economics of Good and Evil: The Quest for Economic Meaning from Gilgamesh to Wall Street* (2011) questions the view of economics as a value-free mathematical inquiry, and instead describes economics as a cultural phenomenon that is deeply interwoven with societal values.

Arjen Kleinherenbrink: Your Economics of Good and Evil *shows how our current economic system relies on a series of foundational beliefs, whose origins you trace to old (often even ancient) philosophies, myths and religious texts. To get started, I would like to ask what drove you to write such a book. Or, to repeat a question you pose in the book, what are old stories, Babylonian myths and New Testament parables good for? What good can they do for us in a time of debt crisis?*

Tomáš Sedláček: Old stories always fascinated me to the same extent that new ones do. I look for the story that is behind mathematics. I enjoy tracing the origins of thoughts and, back in the day, people expressed underlying invisible structures in the terminology of myths. Today we do the same thing, but our underlying principle, our "other world," is composed of mathematical structures. I don't understand the word myth in the sense of something untrue that many believe in, but myth as a looking glass, the matrix through which we see, interpret and understand the world. We don't really look at the matrix, we see through the matrix, the unreal "spiritual" or "intellectual" matrix makes the real really real. A good example of that is money – itself a non-existing, virtual, spiritual entity – which allows us to structure, organize, (e)valuate, validate, relate and compare the world around us. Or the term debt, which in the original Greek means guilt, or sin. The verbatim translation of The Lord's Prayer is "forgive us our debts, as we forgive those who are indebted to us." Debt does not merely have an economic dimension, in fact, psychologically it is similar to sin: forgivable in small one-off quantities, but able to bankrupt you if the imbalance is sustained for too long. So, in short, I think it's really useful to compare the old with the new. Underneath the mathematical cover, there is a realm of myths even in economics. Tracing these myths from the epic of Gilgamesh up to Wall Street – that was what I set out to do in *Economics of Good and Evil*.

AK: In that book, you write that the 2007-2008 financial crisis is not a monetary crisis of the euro, but a crisis of debt. You also call our time the "Debt Age." What, in your view, are the main features and causes of this crisis, on both an individual and a collective level?

TS: So, this follows on nicely from the previous question. Let's take, for a change, the interest rate as an example. In all ancient texts, quite surprisingly for such a technical topic, the interest rate appears as an ethical, alas religious!, issue. In the Vedas, Aristotle, the Bible, the Koran, even the Code of Hammurabi – in all of these, we hear a warning against the fervent usage of the interest rate, not only in case of usury, but all these texts are negative toward the very idea of "charging money for time," as Aristotle puts it. Today we consider the interest rate to be one of the most fundamental and important issues that lies at the very heart of economics, it's considered a purely economic topic. But just because we can measure it precisely doesn't mean that we understand what's going on and what kind of beast we are gleefully driving until it goes wild. Use interest with caution, is the echo of the ancient texts, [yet] we drive it like crazy exactly because we can measure it. And then comes the collapse that Aristotle could easily see, but not us, for we have too much expertise. Credit crunch, after all, means faith crunch, when translated from Latin. We are living in a period of a crisis of faith. We don't know what to believe about the markets. And the euro has little to do with the crisis – this crisis is not monetary, but fiscal.

AK: You write about ancient measures to prevent debts from becoming overly burdensome (jubilee years, for example). You also call attention to how the invention of interest seems to have coincided with the invention of annulling debt. This points to an intertwinement of economics and ethics of a kind that seems to have all but disappeared in contemporary economic theory. What does economics stand to gain with a possible reappreciation of this ethical dimension, for example by acknowledging the deep relations between debt, sin and redemption?

TS: So, this is a *moral* obligation, this "debts *should be* paid back" as David Graeber points out. On this moral imperative, much of our society is built. But how much we need forgiveness (of debt/sin) for our system to work is evident for everybody who reads the newspapers. "Banks will be redeemed" or saved, bailed out, otherwise there will be a financial Armageddon which will burn us all. This is very strong religious language which is used here! Don't forget that forgiveness of debt/sins is one of the key principles of Christianity. We thought that it was "only" an ancient, weird spiritual issue which had nothing to do with our technical/economic Western educated world. But alas, that's exactly what happened. Let me expand on your point that not all debt is equal. Again, an example: there is a 2000-year-old parable in which Jesus talks about a servant who owed the king a ridiculously large debt, in the order of a country's GDP. He is unable to pay it back, so the king forgives him. The servant then meets his own creditor, who owes him approximately one month's wages and he beats him up as he tries to extract the debt from him. Now the king hears of this and has him cast into prison for life, "I forgave you so much and you could not forgive such a small amount!" Now, this story seems ancient and absurd, until we realize that it actually took place, legally, in our lifetime, in our sophisticated, scientific, rule-based society and during broad daylight with everyone conscious. Big sums were forgiven to banks, but not a penny of mortgages was written off. I have not read a better description of what actually happened in 2009 than this old parable. Sometimes it's good to think about the core issue, which mathematics sometimes helps to find and sometimes helps to obscure, such as in this case. My trick is to read technical issues mythologically and mythological issues technically.

AK: Yet older approaches to economics were tailored to economic systems that seem much "simpler" than our current global economy. A defining characteristic of our current financial system is its almost mind-numbing complexity. The sheer numbers, entanglements, varieties and operating speeds of financial products, transactions, actors, algorithms and markets are so incredibly vast that they simply defy our understanding. This is why, for example, in Debt: The First 5000 Years, *David Graeber refers to finance and financial systems as being utterly "arcane." Yet at the same time, there are increasing demands for more transparency, accountability and democratic control concerning financial markets and systems. How can such demands ever be met (in theoretical as well as in practical terms) if they concern entities and events that are opaque and unintelligible in principle? Can they have any emancipatory value?*

TS: As Harari nicely puts it in *Homo Deus*, it is not nature, not Divinity, not human reason nor human feelings but algorithms that will guide us and tell us what to do, how things work etc. Previously, we thought that markets would guide us into the future – the markets as a reducer of complexity. When I was studying, they taught us to believe in the divine possibilities of the market, that markets will solve it all. Despite all the voices crying (together paraphrasing Nietzsche): "the god of the market is dead, he never existed, we wished him into belief" I think that the situation is much more brutal. It's no longer only the "market approach will do it," we went further, we now believe that business approaches will do it. So, in politics, we went even further, the trend in many countries is to ask businesspeople to steer not only the markets, but also politics. Politics has become a cynical, self-centered, ideals-free realm. Just like business predominantly was some two generations ago. Our politicians very often have become professional cynics, they took cynicism professionally and tried to empty it of higher callings and morality.

AK: You also seem to discern a crisis internal to economics itself. During the crisis, austerity measures were presented as being grounded in fully objective facts, which corresponds to the self-image of economics as being a science (specifically: modeled after physics). Yet at the same time, you write about how economists function as "priests" or "prophets" who interpret and predict what the Market "wants," and you mention the "religious and emotional zeal" that accompanies many schools of economic thought. What exactly is this "repressed" side of economics and why is it apparently so hard to acknowledge?

TS: I just published a book about the psychoanalysis of economics called *Lilith and the Demons of Capital* together with Oliver Tanzer. In the book, we put the whole field of economics on the Freudian couch and just listened. What does it fear, what does it talk about, what does it not talk about? What and how does it rationalize the world? What does it run to, what are the attractors? What does it fear, what does it suppress? We found many things, such as reality distortions, messiah complex (from which I think I also suffer, I think economists should try to reinvent the economic system for a new, digital economy). We sometimes situate ourselves as the interpreters of the will of the markets, what do the markets want (from us)? Why do they have a sideways mood? Before the crisis, it seemed as if the financial world, together with the academic, knew perfectly well what it was doing and that it had the markets under control. That all the tricks were known. Well, the financial experts came begging the government to interfere. The mantra of the Wall Street melody makers before was: laissez-faire, laissez-passer, governments do not meddle, politicians are stupid and slow, we are clever and fast. With a snap of a finger, this relation completely reversed during the crisis to: please meddle! Please don't let us be! We don't have a clue, you figure this one out – you clever, we stupid. Please react fast, as only you can, the market forces are too slow and as we all know, we will all be dead in the long run (haha – hoho, we are even funny, you see), etc. This is, of course, top irony. Those very markets, the omnipotent engines of our society, that preached that they would help or save everyone and everything, could not help or save themselves. Another thing is also that not only is the economy bipolar, raging between manias and depressions, but economics seems to have developed this property as well. Once, the field of economics was called a dismal science, exactly because it prophesied that the poor would always be poor and the rich would get richer (see, most notably, Thomas Malthus). This dark prophecy led, later on, to Marxism.

AK: For many theorists, Marxism or Marx-inspired thought is important or even necessary for the analysis of our current economic predicaments and the conceptualization of viable improvements or alternatives to the current economic system. You, however, seem much more inclined to place Marx on the side of the problem rather than the solution. Could you explain how Marxism then actually contributes to the features of economic thought that you deem objectionable?

TS: Marx is a difficult case for me, I'm too emotional about it. Marxism ravaged my country for decades, leaving it almost in ruins economically, mentally, ecologically and politically. I know very well that Marx himself was not a Marxist, but nevertheless, I'm biased. There is not one country in which this attempt was successful, all countries who were inspired by Marx ended as totalitarian states. The only reason China is doing better economically is because they are walking away from Marx. If you read the demands of Marx in the *Communist Manifesto*, they have these ten goals that they wish to achieve. Most of the ones that still make some sense today are actually better fulfilled in European capitalist countries than in communist ones. A worker is much better off here. Another way of looking at it is to say that today in Europe we have incorporated Marxism into the system of social democracy (now I don't mean as a party but as an idea). Roughly 50 percent of GDP goes through taxation, so half your income you can control, the other, politicians control. If you want to, you can also read it this way. Would there be such a caring social state without Marx? I think so, but of course, it's a "what if" debate. (But most scientific debates are "what if" debates, for example when we calculate free fall, we pretend "as if" there were no air resistance. "What if" thinking and "what if" worlds can be very useful.)

AK: You have said in interviews that we must come to terms with the fact that the total wealth in Western society is sufficient, and that it is time to abandon the belief that more economic growth is always better. What are the sources of this belief, and what would it take to collectively "change our minds"?

TS: I'm not against growth per se, just as I'm not against good weather. What I'm saying, though, is that it is foolish to expect every day to be sunny. The danger of our growth is that it's unsustainable, not only ecologically, but also from within, it's not sustainable economically, we mainly grow by debt. It was this debt-induced growth that led to collapse.

AK: In terms of policy, you propose the introduction of mandatory savings, or what you call "Joseph's rule." Could you explain what this would entail, and how it would ward off the adverse effects of debt-driven economies?

TS: We are basically unable to create budget surpluses, which would make our system robust. What the previous generations did was to sell stability (run deficits, increase debt) in order to buy growth (GDP). And we succeeded! We created a system that can grow really fast, but it's also unstable. What we need to do right now is to start selling growth (budget surpluses, decrease debt) in order to buy stability. Joseph's rule is the first recorded fiscal policy executed in our history. It basically says that in good years, do not eat everything that grows, but save a bit of that energy for bad times. Even the Maastricht rules are completely off here: there is no reason that a government should be allowed to run 3 percent GDP deficits in good times. On the contrary 3 percent deficits are hardly enough for an economy which is in crisis. Joseph's principle comes from Genesis 42 and today we call it cyclically balanced budgets. But Joseph goes further. Instead of government debt as primarily a weapon against crises, Joseph had a "state budget" which itself was in surplus. Today, we don't even have a proper name for this.

AK: In an interview with Der Spiegel, *you also propose that in a free-market democracy, politicians should be deprived of the right and authority to incur debt, much like they no longer have the right to print money. What would be the advantages of such a measure? And to whom, then, would the right to incur sovereign debt be transferred?*

TS: Fiscal policy should go the way of monetary policy. Tax policy and expenditures policy should be 100 percent democratic, but fiscal policy, the "printing of debt" should not. Like monetary policy "the printing of money" is (and should be) a-democratic. We do not vote for our governor, which is good. Our crisis was fiscal, fought with monetary means, not the other way around.

Endnotes

The "Financial" Crisis: Ten Years Later

1. See David Harvey, *A Brief History of Neoliberalism* (Oxford: Oxford University Press, 2005); Wolfgang Streeck, *Buying Time: The Delayed Crisis of Democratic Capitalism*, trans. Patrick Camiller (New York: Verso Books, 2014).

2. Christian Marazzi, *The Violence of Financial Capitalism*, trans. Kristina Lebedeva and Jason Francis McGimsey, (Los Angeles: Semiotext(e), 2011); Greta R. Krippner, "The financialization of the American economy", *Socio-Economic Review* 3 (2005): 173-208; Maurizio Lazzarato, *The Making of Indebted Man. An Essay on the Neoliberal Condition*, trans. Joshua David Jordan (Los Angeles: Semiotext(e), 2012).

3. Philip Mirowski, *Never Let a Serious Crisis Go to Waste: How Neoliberalism Survived the Financial Meltdown* (New York: Verso, 2013).

4. Loïc Wacquant, "Three steps to a historical anthropology of actually existing neoliberalism," *Social Anthropology*, 20 no. 1 (2012): 66-79.

5. Naomi Klein, *The Shock Doctrine* (London: Penguin Books, 2007).

6. For a more detailed explanation, see Wolfgang Streeck, "Why the Euro Divides Europe," *New Left Review* 95 (2015): 5-26.

7. Chantal Mouffe, *For a Left Populism* (London: Verso, 2018).

8. Adam Touze, "Ten years after the financial crisis," published August 2, 2018, https://www.economist.com/books-and-arts/2018/08/02/ten-years-after-the-financial-crisis

9. Thomas Piketty, *Capital in the Twenty-First Century*, trans. Arthur Goldhammer (Cambridge MA: Harvard University Press, 2014).

Chapter 1

1. See Nigel Dodd, *The Social Life of Money* (Princeton: Princeton University Press, 2014), 92.

2. Andrea Vogt, "Italian women whose husbands killed themselves in recession stage march," *The Guardian*, April 30, 2012, https://www.theguardian.com/world/2012/apr/30/italian-women-husbands-recession-march.

3. Dodd, *Social Life of Money*, 92. Also see: Margaret Atwood, *Payback. Debt and the Shadow Side of Wealth* (Toronto: House of Anansi Press, 2008).

4. Such was the thesis of Alvin W. Gouldner's analysis of reciprocity as the basis of social ties: "The Norm of Reciprocity: A Preliminary Statement," *American Sociological Review*, vol. 25, n° 2 (1960).

5. Marcel Mauss, *The Gift. The Form and Reason for Exchange in Archaic Society* (London & New York: Routledge, 1990 [1923-1924]).

6. Particular recognition is extended here to the researchers associated with the *Mouvement anti-utilitariste en science sociale* (MAUSS). See especially: Alain Caillé, *Anthropologie du don. Le tiers paradigme* (Paris : Desclée de Brouwer, 2000); Jacques T. Godbout, *Le don, la dette et l'identité. Homo donator vs homo œconomicus* (Montréal: Boréal, 2000).

7. Karl Polanyi, *The Great Transformation: The Political and Economic Origins of Our Times* (Boston: Beacon Press Books, 1944); Pierre Clastres, *Society Against the State*, trans. Robert Hurley (New York: Zone Books, 1987 [1974]); David Graeber, *Debt: The First 5000 Years* (New York: Melville House, 2011).

8. Marcel Hénaff, *The Price of Truth. Gift, Money and Philosophy*, trans. Jean-Louis Morhange (Stanford: Stanford University Press, 2010).

9. Pierre Bourdieu, *Pascalian Meditations*, trans. Richard Nice (Stanford: Stanford University Press, 2000).

10. Jean François Bissonnette, "Le cadeau empoisonné: Pour une

pharmacologie de la dette," ed. Jean François Bissonnette, Pierre Crétois *et alii.*, *La dette comme rapport social: Liberté ou servitude?* (Lormont: Le Bord de l'eau, 2017), 93-122.

11. Richard Dienst, *The Bonds of Debt. Borrowing Against the Common Good* (New York: Verso, 2011).

12. Michael Hardt & Antonio Negri, *Declaration* (Argo Navis Author Services, 2012).

13. Maurizio Lazzarato, *The Making of the Indebted Man. An Essay on the Neoliberal Condition* (Los Angeles: Semiotext(e), 2012), 24.

14. Frédéric Lordon, *L'intérêt souverain. Essai d'anthropologie économique spinoziste* (Paris: La découverte, 2011).

15. Bourdieu, *Pascalian Meditations*.

16. Friedrich Nietzsche, *On The Genealogy of Morals*, II, 1, trans. Walter Kaufmann (New York: Vintage Books, 1967), 57.

17. Georges Bataille, *The Accursed Share*, vol. 1 *Consumption*, trans. Robert Hurley (New York: Zone Books, 1991 [1967]).

18. Adam Smith, *Theory of Moral Sentiments* (London: 1774), 74.

19. Dodd, *Social Life of Money*, 90.

20. Dodd, *Social Life of Money*, 89.

21. David Graeber, *Debt: The First 5000 Years* (New York: Melville House, 2011), in particular ch. 2, 43-72.

22. Hénaff, *The Price of Truth*.

23. Émile Benveniste, *Indo-European Language and Society*, trans. E. Palmer (London: Faber & Faber, 1973).

24. Lordon, *L'intérêt souverain*, 45-49.

25. Lordon, *L'intérêt souverain*.

26. Pierre Bourdieu, *Le sens pratique* (Paris : Minuit, 1980).

27. Dodd, *Social Life of Money*, 96.

28. Michel Aglietta, *La Monnaie. Entre dettes et souveraineté* (Paris: Odile Jacob, 2016), 12-13.

29. John Locke, *Second Treatise on Government*, ch. V, § 36 *in The Works of John Locke* (London, 1823).

30. There should be no surprise at the discovery that the

etymological root of money ties it directly to indebtedness. *Money* is formed by the Latin mūnus, which refers, to an honorific status to which is tied a duty, or an official responsibility. For example, a leader owes entertainments in return for the benefits he gets. *Mūnus* is granted to someone who fulfills some obligations in return.

31. Graeber, *Debt*, 18.
32. Graeber, *Debt*, 14.
33. Karl Marx, *The Capital*, vol. 1, § 8, trans. Samuel Moore and Edward Aveling (Moscow: Progress Publishers, First English edition of 1887), Online: Marx/Engels Internet Archive (marxists.org) 1995, 1999.
34. Nietzsche, *Genealogy of Morals*, II, § 8, 70.
35. Nietzsche, *Genealogy of Morals*, II, § 11, 76.
36. Nietzsche, *Genealogy of Morals*, II, § 11, 76.
37. Benveniste, *Indo-European Language*.
38. Elettra Stimilli, *The Debt of the Living. Ascesis and Capitalism* (New York: Suny Press, 2017), 30.
39. Dienst, *Bonds of Debt*, 185.
40. Dienst, *Bonds of Debt*, 176.
41. Bataille, *The Accursed Share*.
42. Bataille, *The Accursed Share*, 26.
43. Stimilli, *Debt of the Living*, 17.
44. Bataille, *The Accursed Share*, 25.
45. Lordon, *L'Intérêt souverain*.
46. Mauss, *The Gift*, 53, note 201.

Chapter 2

1. "Household debt (indicator)," OECD, 2017, doi: 10.1787/f03b6469-en.
2. Wolfgang Streeck, *Buying Time: The Delayed Crisis of Democratic Capitalism* (London: Verso, 2014) Epub.
3. Colin Crouch, "Privatised Keynesianism: An Unacknowledged Policy Regime," *The British Journal of Politics and In-*

ternational Relations 11, n° 3 (August 2009): 382-399.

4. Andrew Ross, *Creditocracy: and The Case for Debt Refusal* (New York: OR Books, 2014).

5. Michel Foucault, "The Political Technology of Individuals," in *Technologies of the Self: A Seminar with Michel Foucault*, ed. Luther H. Martin, Huck Gutman and Patrick H. Hutton (Amherst: The University of Massachusetts Press, 1988), 157.

6. Margaret Thatcher, "Speech to National Housebuilding Council" (1988), cited in Daniel Béland, "Framing the Ownership Society: Ideas, Institutions, and Neo-Liberal Social Policy," (Chicago: International Sociological Association, 2005): 18.

7. Manuel B. Aalbers, "The Financialization of Home and the Mortgage Market Crisis," *Competition & Change* 12, n° 2 (June 2008): 152.

8. For a nuanced analysis of the various, context-dependent meanings associated with homeownership in different countries, which examines the connection between welfare state reforms, individual strategies of asset building, and the resulting social divisions, see Richard Ronald, *The Ideology of Home Ownership: Homeowner Societies and the Role of Housing* (Basingstoke: Palgrave Macmillan, 2008).

9. Pierre Bourdieu offers a compelling analysis of the political construction of the private housing market in France in the late 1970s, which certainly applies to other Western countries as well. While it facilitated the growth of the housing market by loosening credit regulations, offering various purchase aids, and defining building norms that set a certain standard of homely living, a dedicated state policy also tapped into the "mythopoetics" of homeownership, the set of positive affects and percepts that surround the "home" and that are thoroughly shaped and produced by the housebuilding and cultural industries. See Pierre Bourdieu, *Les structures*

sociales de l'économie (Paris: Seuil, 2000).

10. John Browne, *Securing a Sustainable Future for Higher Education* (Independent Review of Higher Education Funding & Student Finance, United Kingdom, 2008).

11. The following quote is a telling example of the pedagogical philosophy behind the Browne report: "Higher education matters because it transforms the lives of individuals. On graduating, graduates are more likely to be employed, more likely to enjoy higher wages and better job satisfaction, and more likely to find it easier to move from one job to the next." Browne, *Securing*: 14. Viewing education as a skills-acquisition process allowing students to accumulate "human capital" and develop their employability can be traced back to the Chicago school of economics and particularly to the work of Gary Becker.

12. For a critique of this figure, see Stephen Kemp-King, *The Graduate Premium: Manna, Myth or Plain Mis-selling?* (London: The Intergenerational Foundation, 2016).

13. In 2015, the average student debt in England was 44,500 GBP, in Canada: 28,500 CAD, in Australia: 39,700 AUD, in New Zealand: 50,000 NZD, and in the USA: 35,000 USD. Source: Philip Kirby, "Degrees of Debt; Funding and Finance for Undergraduates in Anglophone Countries," (London: The Sutton Trust, April 2016), 12-13.

14. Paul Langley, "Debt, Discipline and Government: Foreclosure and Forbearance in the Subprime Mortgage Crisis," *Environment and Planning A* 41, n° 6 (2009): 1404-1419.

15. Michel Foucault, *The Birth of Biopolitics: Lectures at the Collège de France, 1978-1979* (Basingstoke: Palgrave Macmillan, 2008), 226.

16. Proponents of this reading of Foucault's work on neoliberalism include Geoffroy de Lagasnerie, *La dernière leçon de Michel Foucault. Sur le néolibéralisme, la théorie et la*

politique (Paris: Fayard, 2012); and Daniel Zamora, "Can We Criticize Foucault?," *Jacobin*, October 12, 2014, https://www.jacobinmag.com/2014/12/foucault-interview/.

17. Gilles Deleuze, "Postscript on the Societies of Control," *October* 59 (Winter 1992): 4.

18. Gilles Deleuze, "Postscript": 7.

19. Andrew Ross, *Creditocracy*, 24.

20. Marion Fourcade and Kieran Healy, "Classification situations: Life-chances in the neoliberal era," *Accounting, Organizations and Society* 38, n° 8 (November 2013): 559-572.

Chapter 3

1. Henry David Thoreau, *The Journal 1837-1861*, ed. John R. Stilgoe (New York: New York Review Books, 2009), 30.

2. Fredric Jameson, *Marxism and Form* (Princeton: Princeton University Press, 1971), 129.

3. Ibid., 133.

4. Karl Marx, "Critique of the Gotha Programme," in *The First International and After*, ed. David Fernbach (New York: Vintage Books, 1974), 347.

5. Gilles Deleuze, *Expressionism in Philosophy: Spinoza*, trans. Martin Joughin (New York: Zone Books, 1990), 269.

6. Bertolt Brecht, *Bertolt Brecht's Me-ti: Book of Interventions in the Flow of Things*, ed. and trans. Antony Tatlow (London: Bloomsbury, 2016), 179.

7. Theodor Adorno, *Minima Moralia*, trans. E.F.N. Jephcott (London: Verso Books, 1974), 156. This famous passage carries an unmistakable echo of the equally famous fragment of Epicurus: "The cry of the flesh: not to be hungry, not to be thirsty, not to be cold. For if someone has these things and is confident of having them in the future, he might contend even with <Zeus> for happiness." See Epicurus, *The Epicurus Reader*, trans. and ed. by Brad Inwood and L.P. Gerson (Indianapolis/Cambridge: Hackett Publishing, 1994), 38. I

will return to Epicurus later.

8. Jacques Rancière, *The Emancipated Spectator*, trans. Gregory Elliott (London/New York: Verso, 2011), 49.

9. David Graeber, *The Democracy Project: A History, a Crisis, a Movement* (New York: Spiegel & Grau, 2013), 294.

10. Thomas More, *Utopia, in Three Modern Utopias*, ed. Susan Bruce (Oxford/New York: Oxford University Press, 1999), 68.

11. Ibid., 57.

12. Ibid., 58.

13. Edward Bellamy, *Looking Backward 2000-1887* (New York: Penguin, 1994), 113.

14. Ibid., 107.

15. Ibid., 110.

16. William Morris, *News from Nowhere* (New York: Penguin, 1994), 267.

17. Perry Anderson, "The River of Time," *New Left Review*, II/26 (March/April, 2004), 71.

18. Epicurus, "The Principle Doctrines" in *The Epicurus Reader*, op. cit., 34.

Chapter 4

1. Thomas Hobbes, *Leviathan* (Cambridge: Cambridge University Press, 1996), 89.

2. See Peter R. Sedgwick, "Hobbes, Sovereign Power and Money," in Laurent Milesi, Christopher Müller and Aidan Tynan (eds), *Credo Credit Crisis: Speculations on Faith and Money* (London: Rowman & Littlefield International, 2017), 46.

3. See Simone Weil, *The Need for Roots* trans. A.F. Wills (London: Routledge & Kegan Paul, 1952), 95-96.

4. See David Graeber, *Debt: The First 5000 Years* (New York: Melville, 2011), ch. 9.

5. Notice that where Nietzsche famously derived debt from

the exercise of force, this account derives political power itself from sovereign debt. See Friedrich Nietzsche, *On the Genealogy of Morality*, trans. Carol Diethe (Cambridge: Cambridge University Press, 1994), 41-43.

6. For a brief account of the wider context, see Niall Ferguson, *The Cash Nexus* (London: Penguin, 2001), 111-118.

7. See Craig Muldrew, *The Economy of Obligation* (Basingstoke: Palgrave, 1998).

8. All the preceding details and figures are taken from Daniel Defoe, *An Essay on the South Sea Trade* (London: J. Baker, 1711).

9. Defoe, who regarded his primary duty as a citizen to defend "publick credit", still argued that the financing scheme was viable after the South Sea stock collapsed in 1720. See Defoe, *The South Sea Company Examin'd* (London: J. Roberts, 1720).

10. For the success of the Bank of England in contrast to the South Sea Company at managing public debt, see Andreas Andréadès, *History of the Bank of England 1640-1903* (London: Frank Cass, 1966).

11. See Maurizio Lazzarato, *The Making of Indebted Man* (New York: Semiotext(e), 2011).

12. As Hobbes pointed out, reputation for power is power, *Leviathan* 62; likewise, reputation for creditworthiness is creditworthiness.

13. Philip Coggan, *Paper Promises: Money, Debt and the New World Order* (London: Allen Lane, 2011), 134-135.

14. Cited in Steve Keen, *Can We Avoid Another Financial Crisis?* (Cambridge: Polity, 2017), 115.

15. Keen, *Can We Avoid Another Financial Crisis?*, 56.

16. Keen, *Can We Avoid Another Financial Crisis?*, 81.

Chapter 5

1. Gilles Deleuze, *Negotiations: 1972-1990*, trans. Martin Joughin (New York: Columbia University Press, 1995), 177.

2. Ibid, 178.
3. Ibidem.
4. Ibid, 178-179.
5. Ibid, 180.
6. Ibid, 179-180.
7. Ibid, 180.
8. Marshall McLuhan and Quentin Fiore, *The Medium is the Massage* (New York: Bantam, 1967), 26.
9. Deleuze, *Negotiations*, 180.
10. Ibidem.
11. David Harvey, *The Condition of Postmodernity* (Cambridge: Blackwell, 1990), 141-172.
12. Luc Boltanski and Eve Chiapello, *The New Spirit of Capitalism*, trans. Gregory Elliott (New York: Verso, 2007), 108-121.
13. Giovanni Arrighi, *The Long Twentieth Century: Money, Power, and the Origins of Our Times.* (New York: Verso, 1994), 6.
14. Michael Hardt and Antonio Negri. *Empire* (Cambridge: Harvard University Press, 2001), 254-256.
15. Michel Foucault, *The Birth of Biopolitics (Lectures at the College De France)*, trans. Graham Burchell (New York: Palgrave Macmillan, 2008).
16. Ibid, 15-16.
17. Ibid, 1-2.
18. Ibid, 225.
19. Ibid, 118-119.
20. Ibid, 226.
21. Ibid, 240.
22. Ibid, 243.
23. Ibid, 244.
24. Ibid, 268.
25. Ibid, 269.
26. Ibid, 225.
27. Ibid, 259.
28. Ibid, 259-260.

29. Louis Althusser, *For Marx*, trans. Ben Brewster. (New York: Verso, 2006), 113.

30. Deleuze, *Negotiations*, 181.

Chapter 6

1. See Friedrich Nietzsche, "Zur Genealogie der Moral [1887]," in *Werke*, Bd. VI, 2 (Berlin: Walter de Gruyter, 1968).

2. See Michel Aglietta & André Orléan, *La violence de la monnaie* (Paris: Presses universitaires de France, 1982).

3. See René Girard, *La violence et le sacré* (Paris: Éditions Bernard Grasset, 1972).

4. See Anna Simone, *Suicidi. Studio sulla condizione umana nella crisi [Suicides. A study of the human condition during the financial crisis]* (Milan: Mimesis, 2014).

5. On this issue and more generally in relation to the link between "debt" and "guilt" I shall make reference to my own work: Elettra Stimilli, *Debt and Guilt. A Political Philosophy*, (London: Bloomsbury, 2018).

6. See at least Gary S. Becker, *Human Capital. A Theoretical and Empirical Analysis, with Special Reference to Education* (Chicago/London: The University of Chicago Press,1964); Id., *The Economic Approach to Human Behavior* (Chicago/London: The University of Chicago Press, 1976).

7. In the sense of Michel Foucault: s. *The Birth of Biopolitics; Lectures at the Collège de France, 1978-79*, trans. Graham Burchell (New York: Palgrave Macmillan, 2008), 226.

8. See Ulrich Bröckling, *Das unternehmerische Selbst. Soziologie einer Subjektivierung* (Frankfurt: Suhrkamp, Frankfurt a. M, 2007).

9. See Paolo Virno, *Grammar of the multitude. For an analysis of contemporary forms of life* (New York: Semiotexte, 2012).

10. Walter Benjamin, "Capitalismus als Religion" in, Ibid, *Gesammelte Schriften*, Bd. VI, edited by Rolf Tiedemann and Hermann Schweppenhäuser (Frankfurt a. M.: Suhrkamp,

1974-1989), 100-103. In relation to this text, see the collection of essays Mauro Ponzi, Sarah Scheibenberger, Dario Gentili, Elettra Stimilli (eds.) *Der Kult des Kapitals. Kapitalismus und Religion bei Walter Benjamin* (Heidelberg: Winter Verlag, 2017). (An earlier edition of the book, different from the German edition, was previously published in Italian: Dario Gentili, Mauro Ponzi, Elettra Stimilli, *Il culto del capitale. Walter Benjamin: capitalismo e religione*, (Macerata: Quodlibet, 2014).)

11. See Max Weber, *Gesammelte Aufsätze zur Religionssoziologie* (Tübingen: Möhr, 1920-1921).

12. See Max Weber, *Die protestantische Ethik und der Geist des Kapitalismus, Vollständige Ausgabe*, edited by von Dirk Kaesler, Beck, München, 2010.

13. Walter Benjamin, *Capitalismus als Religion*, ibid, 102.

14. For a more detailed discussion of this point, please see Elettra Stimilli, *The Debt of the Living. Asceticism and Capitalism* (New York: Suny Press, 2017).

15. See Michel Foucault, *Sécurité, territoire, population. Cours au Collège de France 1977-1978* (Paris: Gallimard-Seuil, 2004).

16. See Ibid, *Naissance de la biopolitique. Cours au Collège de France 1978-1979* (Paris: Gallimard-Seuil, 2004).

17. Ibidem, 170.

18. Raymond E. Brown, "The Pater Noster as an Eschatological Prayer," in *New Testament Essays* (Milwaukee, WI: Bruce, 1965), 244.

19. See Gary Anderson, *Sin. A History* (New Haven, CT: Yale University Press, 2009).

20. Paolo Napoli, "*Das* Depositum. *Genealogie eines Verwaltungsarchetyps*," in *Der Kult des Kapitals*, ibid, 249 (117 of the Italian edition).

21. Ibidem, 252 (120 in the Italian edition).

22. Ibidem, 253 (120 in the Italian edition).

23. Ibidem, (ibidem in the Italian edition).

24. Ibidem, 239 (108 in the Italian edition).
25. Ibidem, 246 (114 in the Italian edition).
26. Ibidem, 253 (120 in the Italian edition).
27. Ibidem, 256 (124 in the Italian edition).
28. Ibidem, 258 (124 in the Italian edition).
29. See, for example, the interesting article by Michel Senellart, "Michel Foucault: une autre histoire du christianisme?," *Bulletin di centre d'études médiévales d'Auxerre*, no. 7 (2013), http://cem.revues.org/12872.
30. With regard to this passage, see the analysis of Michel Foucault, *Naissance de la biopolitique*, Ibid, pp. 81 et seq.
31. Oswald von Nell-Breuning, "Neoliberismus und katholische Soziallehre," in *Der Christ und die soziale Marktwirtschaft*, edited by Patrick Boarman, (Stuttgart-Cologne: Kohlhammer, 1955), 101-122.
32. See Jean-Claude Juncker in conversation with Michael Sauga and Christoph Schult, "Athen ist nicht pleite," in *Der Spiegel*, 21 (2011), 64-67.
33. For an interesting analysis of the unification of Germany in relation to the European crisis, see Vladimiro Giacché, *Anschluss. L'annessione. L'unificazione della Germania e il futuro dell'Europa (The Annexation. The unification of Germany and the future of Europe)*, (Reggio Emilia: Imprimator Editore, 2013).
34. Michael Bröcker, Eva Quadbeck, "Wir brauchen eine EU-Treuhand für Griechenland," interview with Frank-Walter Steinmeier, *Rheinische Post*, October 1, 2011.
35. See "Merkel nennt Ostdeutschland Vorbild für Griechenland," in *Zeit Online*, October 5, 2011.

Chapter 10

1. The interview was conducted over the phone by Bordeleau and included questions from both Bordeleau and van Tuinen.

References

The "Financial" Crisis: Ten Years Later

Harvey, David. *A Brief History of Neoliberalism*. Oxford: Oxford University Press, 2015.

Klein, Naomi. *The Shock Doctrine*. London: Penguin Books, 2007.

Krippner, Greta R. "The financialization of the American economy." *Socio-Economic Review* 3 (2005): 173-208.

Lazzarato, Maurizio. *The Making of Indebted Man. An Essay on the Neoliberal Condition*. Translated by Joshua David Jordan. Los Angeles: Semiotext(e), 2012.

Marazzi, Christian. *The Violence of Financial Capitalism*. Translated by Kristina Lebedeva and Jason Francis McGimsey. Los Angeles: Semiotext(e), 2011.

Mouffe, Chantal. *For a Left Populis*. London: Verso, 2018.

Mirowski, Philip. *Never Let a Serious Crisis Go to Waste: How Neoliberalism Survived the Financial Meltdown*. New York: Verso, 2013.

Piketty, Thomas. *Capital in the Twenty-First Century*, trans. Arthur Goldhammer. Cambridge MA: Harvard University Press, 2014.

Streeck, Wolfgang. *Buying Time: The Delayed Crisis of Democratic Capitalism*. Translated by Patrick Camiller. New York: Verso Books, 2014.

Streeck, Wolfgang. "Why the Euro Divides Europe," *New Left Review* 95 (2015): 5-26.

Touze, Adam. "Ten years after the financial crisis," published August 2, 2018, https://www.economist.com/books-and-arts/2018/08/02/ten-years-after-the-financial-crisis

Wacquant, Loïc. "Three steps to a historical anthropology of actually existing neoliberalism," *Social Anthropology*, 20 no. 1 (2012): 66-79.

Chapter 1

Aglietta, Michel. *La Monnaie. Entre dettes et souveraineté*. Paris: Odile Jacob, 2016.

Atwood, Margaret. *Payback. Debt and the Shadow Side of Wealth*. Toronto: House of Anansi Press, 2008.

Bataille, Georges. *The Accursed Share*, vol. 1 *Consumption*, trans. Robert Hurley. New York: Zone Books, 1991 [1967].

Benveniste, Émile. *Indo-European Language and Society*, trans. E. Palmer. London: Faber & Faber, 1973.

Bissonnette, Jean François. "Le cadeau empoisonné: Pour une pharmacologie de la dette," ed. Jean François Bissonnette, Pierre Crétois *et alii.*, *La dette comme rapport social: Liberté ou servitude?* Lormont: Le Bord de l'eau, 2017.

Bourdieu, Pierre. *Le sens pratique*. Paris: Minuit, 1980.

Bourdieu, Pierre. *Pascalian Meditations*, trans. Richard Nice. Stanford: Stanford University Press, 2000.

Caillé, Alain. *Anthropologie du don. Le tiers paradigme*. Paris: Desclée de Brouwer, 2000.

Clastres, Pierre. *Society Against the State*, trans. Robert Hurley. New York: Zone Books, 1987 [1974].

Dienst, Richard. *The Bonds of Debt. Borrowing Against the Common Good*. New York: Verso, 2011.

Dodd, Nigel. *The Social Life of Money*. Princeton: Princeton University Press, 2014.

Godbout, Jacquet T. *Le don, la dette et l'identité. Homo donator vs homo œconomicus*. Montréal: Boréal, 2000.

Gouldner, Alvin W. "The Norm of Reciprocity: A Preliminary Statement," *American Sociological Review*, vol. 25, n°2 (1960).

Graeber, David. *Debt: The First 5000 Years*. New York: Melville House, 2011.

Hardt, Michael & Negri, Antonio. *Declaration*. Argo Navis Author Services, 2012.

Hénaff, Marcel. *The Price of Truth. Gift, Money and Philosophy*, trans. Jean-Louis Morhange. Stanford: Stanford University

Press, 2010.

Lazzarato, Maurizio. *The Making of the Indebted Man. An Essay on the Neoliberal Condition.* Los Angeles: Semiotext(e), 2012.

Locke, John. *Second Treatise on Government*, ch. V, § 36 *in The Works of John Locke.* London, 1823.

Lordon, Frédéric. *L'intérêt souverain. Essai d'anthropologie économique spinoziste.* Paris: La découverte, 2011.

Marx, Karl. *The Capital*, vol. 1, § 8, trans. Samuel Moore and Edward Aveling. Moscow: Progress Publishers, First English edition of 1887, Online: Marx/Engels Internet Archive (marxists.org) 1995, 1999.

Mauss, Marcel. *The Gift. The Form and Reason for Exchange in Archaic Society.* London & New York: Routledge, 1990 [1923-1924].

Nietzsche, Friedrich. *On The Genealogy of Morals*, II, 1, trans. Walter Kaufmann. New York: Vintage Books, 1967.

Polanyi, Karl. *The Great Transformation: The Political and Economic Origins of Our Times.* Boston: Beacon Press Books, 1944.

Smith, Adam. *Theory of Moral Sentiments.* London: 1774.

Stimilli, Elettra. *The Debt of the Living. Ascesis and Capitalism.* New York: Suny Press, 2017.

Vogt, Andrea. "Italian women whose husbands killed themselves in recession stage march," *The Guardian*, April 30, 2012, https://www.theguardian.com/world/2012/apr/30/italian-women-husbands-recession-march.

Chapter 2

Aalbers, Manuel B. "The Financialization of Home and the Mortgage Market Crisis." *Competition & Change* 12, n° 2 (June 2008): 148-166.

Béland, Daniel. "Framing the Ownership Society: Ideas, Institutions, and Neo-Liberal Social Policy." Chicago: International Sociological Association, 2005.

Bourdieu, Pierre. *Les structures sociales de l'économie.* Paris: Seuil,

2000.

Browne, John. *Securing a Sustainable Future for Higher Education*. Independent Review of Higher Education Funding & Student Finance, United Kingdom, 2008.

Crouch, Colin. "Privatised Keynesianism: An Unacknowledged Policy Regime." *The British Journal of Politics and International Relations* 11, n° 3 (August 2009): 382-399.

De Lagasnerie, Geoffroy. *La dernière leçon de Michel Foucault. Sur le néolibéralisme, la théorie et la politique*. Paris: Fayard, 2012.

Deleuze, Gilles. "Postscript on the Societies of Control." *October* 59 (Winter 1992): 3-7.

Foucault, Michel. "The Political Technology of Individuals." In *Technologies of the Self: A Seminar with Michel Foucault*, edited by Luther H. Martin, Huck Gutman and Patrick H. Hutton, 145-162. Amherst: The University of Massachusetts Press, 1988.

Foucault, Michel. *The Birth of Biopolitics: Lectures at the Collège de France, 1978-1979*. Basingstoke: Palgrave Macmillan, 2008.

Fourcade, Marion, and Kieran Healy. "Classification situations: Life-chances in the neoliberal era." *Accounting, Organizations and Society* 38, n° 8 (November 2013): 559-572.

Kemp-King, Stephen. *The Graduate Premium: Manna, Myth or Plain Mis-selling?* London: The Intergenerational Foundation, 2016.

Kirby, Philip. *Degrees of Debt; Funding and Finance for Undergraduates in Anglophone Countries*. London: The Sutton Trust, April 2016.

Langley, Paul. "Debt, Discipline and Government: Foreclosure and Forbearance in the Subprime Mortgage Crisis." *Environment and Planning A* 41, n° 6 (2009): 1404-1419.

OECD. "Household debt (indicator)," 2017, doi: 10.1787/f03b6469-en.

Ronald, Richard. *The Ideology of Home Ownership: Homeowner Societies and the Role of Housing*. Basingstoke: Palgrave

Macmillan, 2008.

Ross, Andrew. *Creditocracy: and The Case for Debt Refusal.* New York: OR Books, 2014.

Streeck, Wolfgang. *Buying Time: The Delayed Crisis of Democratic Capitalism.* London: Verso, 2014. Epub.

Zamora, Daniel. "Can We Criticize Foucault?" *Jacobin,* October 12, 2014, https://www.jacobinmag.com/2014/12/foucault-interview/

Chapter 4

Andréadès, Andreas. *History of the Bank of England 1640-1903.* London: Frank Cass, 1966.

Coggan, Philip. *Paper Promises: Money, Debt and the New World Order.* London: Allen Lane, 2011.

Defoe, Daniel. *An Essay on the South Sea Trade.* London: J. Baker, 1711.

Defoe, Daniel. *The South Sea Company Examin'd.* London: J. Roberts, 1720.

Ferguson, Niall. *The Cash Nexus.* London: Penguin, 2001.

Graeber, David. *Debt: The First 5000 Years.* New York: Melville, 2011.

Hobbes, Thomas. *Leviathan.* Cambridge: Cambridge University Press, 1996.

Keen, Steve. *Can We Avoid Another Financial Crisis?* Cambridge: Polity, 2017.

Lazzarato, Maurizio. *The Making of Indebted Man.* New York: Semiotext(e), 2011.

Muldrew, Craig. *The Economy of Obligation.* Basingstoke: Palgrave, 1998.

Nietzsche, Friedrich. *On the Genealogy of Morality,* trans. Carol Diethe. Cambridge: Cambridge University Press, 1994.

Sedgwick, Peter R. "Hobbes, Sovereign Power and Money", in Laurent Milesi, Christopher Müller, and Aidan Tynan (eds), *Credo Credit Crisis: Speculations on Faith and Money.* London:

Rowman & Littlefield International, 2017.

Weil, Simone. *The Need for Roots* trans. A.F. Wills. London: Routledge & Kegan Paul, 1952.

Chapter 5

Althusser, Louis. *For Marx*. Trans. Ben Brewster. New York: Verso, 2006.

Arrighi, Giovanni. *The Long Twentieth Century: Money, Power, and the Origins of Our Times*. New York: Verso, 1994.

Boltanski, Luc and Eve Chiapello. *The New Spirit of Capitalism*. Trans. Gregory Elliott. New York: Verso, 2007.

Deleuze, Gilles. *Negotiations 1972-1990*. Trans. Martin Joughin. New York: Columbia University Press, 1995.

Foucault, Michel. *The Birth of Biopolitics (Lectures at the College De France)*. Trans. Graham Burchell. New York: Palgrave Macmillan, 2008.

Hardt, Michael and Antonio Negri. *Empire*. Cambridge: Harvard University Press, 2001.

Harvey, David. *The Condition of Postmodernity*. Cambridge: Blackwell, 1990.

McLuhan, Marshall and Quentin Fiore. *The Medium is the Massage*. New York: Bantam, 1967.

Chapter 6

Aglietta, Michel & André Orléan. *La violence de la monnaie.* Paris: Presses universitaires de France, 1982.

Anderson, Gary. *Sin. A History*. New Haven, CT: Yale University Press, 2009.

Becker, Gary S. *Human Capital. A Theoretical and Empirical Analysis, with Special Reference to Education*. Chicago/London: The University of Chicago Press, 1964.

Becker, Gary S. *The Economic Approach to Human Behavior*. Chicago/London: The University of Chicago Press, 1976.

Benjamin, Walter. "Capitalismus als Religion" in, Ibid,

Gesammelte Schriften, Bd. VI, edited by Rolf Tiedemann and Hermann Schweppenhäuser. Frankfurt a. M.: Suhrkamp, 1974-1989.

Bröcker, Michael and Eva Quadbeck. "Wir brauchen eine EU-Treuhand für Griechenland," interview with Frank-Steinmeier, Walter *Rheinische Post*, October 1, 2011.

Bröckling, Ulrich. *Das unternehmerische Selbst. Soziologie einer Subjektivierung*. Frankfurt: Suhrkamp, Frankfurt a. M, 2007.

Brown, Raymond E. "The Pater Noster as an Eschatological Prayer," in *New Testament Essays*. Milwaukee, WI: Bruce, 1965.

Foucault, Michel. *The Birth of Biopolitics; Lectures at the Collège de France, 1978-79*, trans. Graham Burchell. New York: Palgrave Macmillan, 2008. Translated from Michel Foucault. *Naissance de la biopolitique. Cours au Collège de France 1978-1979*. Paris: Gallimard-Seuil, 2004.

Foucault, Michel. *Sécurité, territoire, population. Cours au Collège de France 1977-1978*. Paris: Gallimard-Seuil, 2004.

Giacché, Vladimiro. *Anschluss. L'annessione. L'unificazione della Germania e il futuro dell'Europa (The Annexation. The unification of Germany and the future of Europe)*, Reggio Emilia: Imprimator Editore, 2013.

Girard, René. *La violence et le sacré*. Paris: Éditions Bernard Grasset, 1972.

Napoli, Paolo. "*Das* Depositum. *Genealogie eines Verwaltungsarchetyps*," in Ponzi, Mauro, Sarah Scheibenberger, Dario Gentili, Elettra Stimilli (eds.) *Der Kult des Kapitals. Kapitalismus und Religion bei Walter Benjamin*. Heidelberg: Winter Verlag, 2017.

Nell-Breuning, Oswald von. "Neoliberismus und katholische Soziallehre," in *Der Christ und die soziale Marktwirtschaft*, edited by Patrick Boarman. Stuttgart-Cologne: Kohlhammer, 1955, 101-122.

Nietzsche, Friedrich. "Zur Genealogie der Moral [1887]," in *Werke*, Bd. VI, 2. Berlin: Walter de Gruyter, 1968.

Ponzi, Mauro, Sarah Scheibenberger, Dario Gentili, Elettra Stimilli (eds.) *Der Kult des Kapitals. Kapitalismus und Religion bei Walter Benjamin*. Heidelberg: Winter Verlag, 2017. Translated from: Dario Gentili, Mauro Ponzi, Elettra Stimilli, *Il culto del capitale. Walter Benjamin: capitalismo e religione*, Macerata: Quodlibet, 2014.

Sauga, Michael and Christoph Schult, "Athen ist nicht pleite," in *Der Spiegel*, 21 (2011), 64-67.

Senellart, Michel. "Michel Foucault: une autre histoire du christianisme?," *Bulletin di centre d'études médiévales d'Auxerre*, no. 7 (2013), http://cem.revues.org/12872.

Simone, Anna. *Suicidi. Studio sulla condizione umana nella crisi [Suicides. A study of the human condition during the financial crisis]*. Milan: Mimesis, 2014.

Stimilli, Elettra. *Debt and Guilt. A Political Philosophy*. London: Bloomsbury, 2018.

Stimilli, Elettra. *The Debt of the Living. Asceticism and Capitalism*. New York: SUNY Press, 2017.

Virno, Paolo. *Grammar of the multitude. For an analysis of contemporary forms of life*. New York: Semiotext(e), 2012.

Weber, Max. *Gesammelte Aufsätze zur Religionssoziologie*. Tübingen: Möhr, 1920-1921.

Weber, Max. *Die protestantische Ethik und der Geist des Kapitalismus, Vollständige Ausgabe*, edited by von Dirk Kaesler. München: Beck, 2010.

Zeit Online. *Merkel nennt Ostdeutschland Vorbild für Griechenland*. October 5, 2011.

CULTURE, SOCIETY & POLITICS

Contemporary culture has eliminated the concept and public
figure of the intellectual. A cretinous anti-intellectualism
presides, cheer-led by hacks in the pay of multinational
corporations who reassure their bored readers that there is no
need to rouse themselves from their stupor. Zer0 Books knows
that another kind of discourse – intellectual without being
academic, popular without being populist – is not only possible:
it is already flourishing. Zer0 is convinced that in the unthinking,
blandly consensual culture in which we live, critical and engaged
theoretical reflection is more important than ever before.
If you have enjoyed this book, why not tell other readers by
posting a review on your preferred book site.

Recent bestsellers from Zero Books are:

In the Dust of This Planet
Horror of Philosophy vol. 1
Eugene Thacker
In the first of a series of three books on the Horror of Philosophy,
In the Dust of This Planet offers the genre of horror as a way of
thinking about the unthinkable.
Paperback: 978-1-84694-676-9 ebook: 978-1-78099-010-1

Capitalist Realism
Is there no alternative?
Mark Fisher
An analysis of the ways in which capitalism has presented itself
as the only realistic political-economic system.
Paperback: 978-1-84694-317-1 ebook: 978-1-78099-734-6

Rebel Rebel
Chris O'Leary
David Bowie: every single song. Everything you want to know,
everything you didn't know.
Paperback: 978-1-78099-244-0 ebook: 978-1-78099-713-1

Cartographies of the Absolute
Alberto Toscano, Jeff Kinkle
An aesthetics of the economy for the twenty-first century.
Paperback: 978-1-78099-275-4 ebook: 978-1-78279-973-3

Romeo and Juliet in Palestine
Teaching Under Occupation
Tom Sperlinger
Life in the West Bank, the nature of pedagogy and the role of a
university under occupation.
Paperback: 978-1-78279-637-4 ebook: 978-1-78279-636-7

Malign Velocities
Accelerationism and Capitalism
Benjamin Noys
Long listed for the Bread and Roses Prize 2015, *Malign Velocities* argues against the need for speed, tracking acceleration as the symptom of the ongoing crises of capitalism.
Paperback: 978-1-78279-300-7 ebook: 978-1-78279-299-4

Meat Market
Female Flesh under Capitalism
Laurie Penny
A feminist dissection of women's bodies as the fleshy fulcrum of capitalist cannibalism, whereby women are both consumers and consumed.
Paperback: 978-1-84694-521-2 ebook: 978-1-84694-782-7

Poor but Sexy
Culture Clashes in Europe East and West
Agata Pyzik
How the East stayed East and the West stayed West.
Paperback: 978-1-78099-394-2 ebook: 978-1-78099-395-9

Sweetening the Pill
or How We Got Hooked on Hormonal Birth Control
Holly Grigg-Spall
Has contraception liberated or oppressed women? *Sweetening the Pill* breaks the silence on the dark side of hormonal contraception.
Paperback: 978-1-78099-607-3 ebook: 978-1-78099-608-0

Why Are We The Good Guys?
Reclaiming your Mind from the Delusions of Propaganda
David Cromwell
A provocative challenge to the standard ideology that Western
power is a benevolent force in the world.
Paperback: 978-1-78099-365-2 ebook: 978-1-78099-366-9

Readers of ebooks can buy or view any of these bestsellers by
clicking on the live link in the title. Most titles are published
in paperback and as an ebook. Paperbacks are available in
traditional bookshops. Both print and ebook formats are available
online.
Find more titles and sign up to our readers' newsletter
at http://www.johnhuntpublishing.com/culture-and-politics
Follow us on Facebook
at https://www.facebook.com/ZeroBooks
and Twitter at https://twitter.com/Zer0Books